Claytie and the Lady

Sue Tolleson-Rinehart
and Jeanie R. Stanley

CLAYTIE
AND THE LADY

Ann Richards, Gender,
and Politics in Texas

UNIVERSITY OF TEXAS PRESS
Austin

Copyright © 1994 by the University of Texas Press
All rights reserved
Printed in the United States of America
First edition, 1994

Requests for permission to reproduce material from this
work should be sent to Permissions, University of Texas
Press, P.O. Box 7819, Austin, TX 78713-7819.

∞The paper used in this publication meets the minimum
requirements of American National Standard for Information
Sciences—Permanence of Paper for Printed Library Materials,
ANSI Z39.48-1984.

Library of Congress Cataloging-in-Publication Data

Tolleson-Rinehart, Sue, date
　　　Claytie and the lady : Ann Richards, gender, and politics
in Texas
　　　　Sue Tolleson-Rinehart, Jeanie R. Stanley. — 1st ed.
　　　　　　p.　　cm.
　　　Includes bibliographical references and index.
　　　ISBN 0-292-77065-0. — ISBN 0-292-77066-9 (pbk.)
　　　1. Texas—Politics and government—1951–　　.
2. Richards, Ann, 1933–　　.　　3. Williams, Clayton,
1931–　　.　　4. Women in politics—Texas—History—
20th century.　　5. Governors—Texas—Election.
　　　I. Stanley, Jeanie Ricketts, date.　　II. Title.
　　　F391.2.T64　　1994　　　　　　　　　　93-48116
　　　976.4′063—dc20

Contents

LIST OF FIGURES AND TABLES

Acknowledgments

Many people deserve our gratitude for the help they have given us from the beginning of this project. The staff and trustees of the John Anson Kittredge Educational Fund provided funding for us to present an initial paper in July 1991 at the Annual Scientific Meeting of the International Society of Political Psychology in Helsinki, Finland, where we quickly saw that the story of the 1990 Texas gubernatorial election had a universal appeal. It was also in Helsinki, as we strolled down a boulevard in the white night, that our friend and colleague M. Margaret Conway told us this *had* to be a book. Here it is, Peggy. We hope you enjoy the end of what you encouraged us to begin!

We wish to extend our deepest thanks to all of the people who graciously permitted us to interview them and to identify them. Their insights were quite simply invaluable.

George Shipley and Royal Masset not only allowed us to interview them, but cheerfully supplied us with a variety of information and answers to our questions. Wayne Slater of the Austin Bureau of the *Dallas Morning News* came to our rescue with data on Clayton Williams' campaign finances, and Jennifer Treat provided a wealth of information on money in Ann Richards' campaign. Candace Wendel of the Texas Poll was also generous to us. Corkie Hilliard and Carol Whitcraft Fredericks were unstinting benefactors of their long and acute observations of Texas politics and public sector management. Jacqueline Maxfield performed the difficult job of transcribing some of our interview tapes with speedy grace. Donna Barnes and Penny McLaughlin in Lubbock were always ready to come to our aid; they have expressed the hope that we will sell even more copies of this book than they have produced on the laser printer. Cliff Rinehart shared his software and his imagination in the production of Figure 4.1. Johnny shared his patience while Mom was writing a book about Lily's grandma. Theresa May of the University of Texas Press has supported the idea of the book from the beginning, and pushed and prodded us along to completion. Carolyn Cates Wylie was a courteously efficient managing editor, and Mandy Woods performed a lovingly careful job of copy-editing.

Two anonymous readers for the University of Texas Press were extraordinarily knowledgeable, cogent in their suggestions, and generous in their praise. When they were revealed to be Janet Boles and Diane Blair, we were not surprised at the wonderfully helpful reviews we had gotten. We thank them for having made this a better book.

All of these people have shown us once again that scholarly creativity is always a collaborative venture. Without their generous help this book would not exist. Without their good humor and enthusiasm, our writing of the book certainly would not have been the scintillating experience they helped to make it.

Finally, we would like to thank Governor Richards and all of the women occupying, or intending to occupy, high political office for putting themselves on the line, and for putting questions of sex and gender in politics to the strongest, most meaningful tests of all.

Claytie and the Lady

With this kind of crisp breeze in the air, I thought, hmm, hmm, it is going to be nice to start wearing some wool suits, and I need to get myself a new pair of shoes . . . This fall, what I want you to do, is write Barbara Boxer and Dianne Feinstein [the Democratic candidates competing to win California's two U.S. Senate seats] a check for just one good pair of Ferragamo shoes. You might even stretch it out to an Ellen Tracy jacket and an Anne Klein pair of slacks. Feel good about yourself!

—GOVERNOR ANN RICHARDS, October 1992, at a Boxer/Feinstein fundraiser in California (Murphy 1992)

The Meaning of the 1990 Gubernatorial Race

Someone once said that Texas is a place where all the women are strong, all the men are weak, and everyone pretends it's the other way around. Whatever we might say about the possible weaknesses of Texas men, Ann Richards certainly showed the strength of Texas women in her grueling 1990 campaign to become the nation's most prominent woman governor (and, except perhaps for New York's Mario Cuomo, the nation's most prominent Governor, period). Her success made her the leader of one part of the women's movement, at least insofar as she became the most visible female elected official. And, as the epigraph suggests, she has taken that role seriously, campaigning in her inimitable style for other women traveling the road to high political office.

But one of us remembers a spring afternoon in Lubbock, Texas, when then State Treasurer Ann Richards stood before a group of (mostly) women, appealing to them for their support in what was shaping up to be a vintage Texas gubernatorial primary campaign: bitter, expensive, and no holds barred. Richards told her audience that day that she had recently gotten a note, along with a check, from an old friend, who said that after looking at what she spent on clothing, she thought, "Is this what I want my daughters to see—that I had a good wardrobe?" The friend wanted her daughters to see something else as well, and so she sent Ann Richards an amount comparable to what she had recently spent on clothes.

At that time, Richards already had attracted an ardent core of supporters to her gubernatorial campaign. What she had *not* been able to attract were the traditional big donors in Texas Democratic politics. The contribution from her friend, and the many small contributions that were sent to the campaign by women everywhere, were heartwarming, but money continued to present harrowing problems to the Richards campaign (problems which we shall be analyzing in detail in Chapter 3).

Paradoxically, one of the consequences of her victory under such difficult conditions was that she later found herself in a position to use what her friend had done, not by then to ask for sums for her own campaign, but, as the nation's best-known female elected official, to enrich the coffers of women running in 1992—the "Year of the Woman," a phenomenon that Richards herself had helped to create by surviving the rigors of 1990.

Ann Richards' electoral triumph made, and makes, a wonderful story. It is full of the color and drama on which Texans pride themselves, and it shows American politics at its grittiest, liveliest, most banal, and most puzzling. It thrilled women across the country (each of us was constantly asked about the campaign by friends and colleagues outside Texas; and Gloria Steinem, addressing a Texas university audience in the spring of 1990, suddenly interrupted herself to say, "You *must* give us Ann Richards [as a Governor]. She's a national treasure."). It provided an unceasing flow of grist for the mills of delighted pundits and journalists. We have had a grand time telling that story in these pages.

But there is much more than a wonderful story to be told. Public, political leadership, in all but a handful of the world's cultures, has been gendered, as has so much else in those cultures. While that has been changing in the United States and elsewhere, and while there have always been ruling queens and women warriors, the woman leader has been an exception, even an aberration, and she has certainly been a "symbolic woman" (see Sapiro 1993). She has been a symbolic woman because she has been unusual, singular: she stands out, even when she emphatically does not want to, as the one who looks different, and she cannot help but trigger questions about what she is doing, how she is doing it, and whether she *can* do it "as well as a man." The epistemology and even the ontology of leadership have been gendered. They have been inextricably associated with masculinity.

Lately, of course, more and more women have entered public office; the last twenty years in the United States have seen steady growth in the number of women in state legislatures, for example, and 1992 produced an almost startling leap in the number of women elected to the U.S. House of Representatives and Senate (although the leap, significant as it was, did not lift women to anywhere near parity in virtual representation). Voters seem more and more inclined of late to believe that women make *better* representatives of certain kinds of interests than do men: women in office are expected to be more accountable, better stewards, more responsive; women in office are thought to be "better" at domestic issues than are men. This perception on the part of voters helps to explain how women's share of state legislative seats has risen from 8% in 1975 to approximately 23% in 1993, and how their share of municipal offices has increased even more (figures from the Center for the American Woman and Politics, Rutgers University).

But even as we contemplate this new acceptance of women in legislative positions, we must remember two very important things. First, the *new* acceptance of women in office emanates from *old* gender-role stereotypes about what women and men do. Politics, even after "years of women," is no farther than it ever was from seeing divisions between the sexes, and from reifying those divisions in beliefs about gender roles. The readiness to accept a "women's" political leadership is new; the belief that women will be different is not.

Second, the acceptance of women in office has only very uneasily been extended to the idea of women as political chief executives. As voters, we still seem more comfortable with women who represent us than we do with women who "run things" (with the possible exception of women who run our cities as mayors), even though many have come to expect that women's leadership would, in this regard, be transformational for politics (see Burns 1978). While women's share of legislative offices of all types has grown steadily, women's share of gubernatorial offices has not. The great period of growth of numbers of women in elective office, beginning in the mid-1970s, is also reflected among governors, but here the change has been that now there actually have been some. Although in 1925 Nellie Tayloe Ross in Wyoming and Miriam

Claytie and the Lady

Ferguson in Texas were inaugurated as surrogates for their husbands (as was Lurleen Wallace of Alabama in the 1960s), it was not until 1975, when Ella Grasso took office as Governor of Connecticut, that a woman came to serve as her state's chief executive after having been elected genuinely in her own right. In less than twenty years, though, seven other women, including Ann Richards, had joined Grasso in the record books; one, Madeleine Kunin of Vermont, was elected to three terms. (One other, Rose Mofford of Arizona, succeeded to the governorship after the incumbent was impeached, but she had been elected Secretary of State in her own right.) In 1990, Richards' victory was accompanied by the victories of Barbara Roberts in Oregon and, perhaps more surprisingly, Joan Finney of Kansas. We can do no more than speculate about *which* woman might make the first race for President as a major party candidate (though, of course, many people have speculated that that woman will be Ann Richards, if on no other basis than her present visibility), much less how she might be received and whether she could win. Certainly, women's recent successes as gubernatorial contestants have broadened such speculation. But it is still here, in the highest offices, among the political chief executives, that sex and gender pose the most complicated challenges, to candidates, voters, and scholars alike. It was just this kind of office that Ann Richards won in 1990—but all three women running for Governor as major party candidates in 1992 were defeated. Women's fortunes as political leaders remain far from settled.

And so, while we tell the wonderful story, the real purpose of this book is to disentangle the effects on the 1990 gubernatorial race of sex and gender roles in the Texas political culture and, in so doing, to aid our understanding of these effects in American politics generally. Beliefs about gender roles, and the application of those beliefs to political decisions, can be quite difficult to quantify; it is particularly easy in these cases to believe that we have indeed found what we expected to find. Casual and even highly motivated observers of the 1990 election might assume, for example, that they had spotted another appearance of the gender gap—that women were supporting Richards, and that men were supporting her Republican opponent, Clayton Williams.

A gender gap did, indeed, cleave the political terrain. But something more interesting than the modal tendency of men and women to cast opposing votes was transpiring. The evidence suggests that in this race, gender-role beliefs both harmed and helped each candidate. Ann Richards was assuredly a role model around whom a devout core of women supporters gathered early on. Had she been a man, in fact, she probably could not have stimulated such fervent early support for her candidacy; nor would such a heavy burden of expectations have been placed on her. But not all women reacted favorably to her or to the idea of women in politics, and some were violently opposed to her: white women as a whole were nearly perfectly divided in their votes for Richards and Williams, especially because, we believe, Ann Richards became a particularly distressing threat to women of her own generation who, unlike Richards, had pursued traditional roles.

Clayton Williams, on the other hand, may have been the last major party candidate in Texas to appeal so openly to its macho cowboy past or, in less flattering terms, to "Bubba." His appeal was gender based, a clarion call to fading visions of frontier masculinity. It won him significant male support (and even the support of some women) but, in the end, it also cost him a victory in circumstances where he would otherwise have been described as the candidate with all the advantages of money, organization, and voters' partisan leanings. His advantages came to naught at least partly because some traditional males to whom his image was appealing were finally put off by his treatment of Ann Richards (the lady) and because more sophisticated men, who would ordinarily vote Republican, were embarrassed by him (as were urban, educated Republican women, who defected to Richards in unusually large numbers).

After its long history as a Democratic bastion, Texas is now a state with vigorous two-party competition, and in the eighties, Republican gubernatorial and presidential candidates have done exceptionally well there. Only two years before the Richards-Williams race, George Bush defeated Michael Dukakis by a solid 56% to 44% margin in the state. In the 1990 gubernatorial campaign, the complications introduced by the paradoxes of gender were among the forces that contributed to Richards' low standing not only in West Texas (where the cowboys are) but, with more serious consequences for the possibility of a Democratic victory, in conservative but usually loyally Democratic East Texas as well. Until the last weeks of the race, Williams held a commanding lead in virtually all private and public polls. Under such circumstances, the race could have been described not as one that Richards won, but as one that Williams lost.

The whole campaign, but especially the general election campaign, became alienating enough to resurrect that old Texas cliché of a choice between the "evil of two lessers," both candidates having been so bruised and bloodied that, for many, neither candidate could be wholeheartedly supported. (Late in the general election campaign season, the following joke was making the rounds: Ann Richards and Clayton Williams were in a boat that capsized. Who was saved? Texas.) If such a state of affairs is an all-too-common phenomenon in Texas politics, gender-role beliefs added a distinctly uncommon—and unpredictable—element to the 1990 race. "It is remarkable that she was elected in a political climate that is supposed to favor conservatives, but this election had nothing to do with liberal-conservative politics. It was a personality contest and a gender contest and a contest of perceptions, and she was perceived to be savvy and more experienced," George Christian, President Johnson's press secretary, told the *New York Times* (Suro 1990) the day after the election.

While that is an oversimplification of a very complicated race, it does capture some important elements of the campaign. Except, perhaps, for those on abortion, liberal and conservative, or Democratic and Republican, policy positions rather rapidly receded into the shadows cast by the candidates' personalities. This is not unusual in American politics. Nor is it an inappropriate or irrational reaction for voters to turn their attention to those personalities: they were, after all, choosing the leader of one of the nation's three largest states, and leaders' personalities and behavior do matter. In such cases, one's perception of a candidate as a potential leader must be based in large part on the *whole* image that the candidate presents (see, for example, Lodge, McGraw, and Stroh 1989). Ann Richards had already established a formidable reputation as a skilled and effective manager, but Clayton Williams depicted himself as a shrewd, tough creator of wealth (a depiction that was to have frayed a good deal around the edges by election day). Who would most successfully appeal to voters in this regard, and how? And what would the prisms of gender have to do with it all?

It is at this point, as candidates are trying to present themselves, and voters are trying to evaluate them, that sex and gender[1] start to matter very much, but in ways that can be extremely challenging to identify with any confidence. Certainly, although most voters claimed in exit polls that the sex of the candidate had not been a determinative factor, it is difficult to believe that it was not. Voters themselves must have been uncomfortably unwilling or unable always to say just *how* the candidates' sex factored into their decisions about Richards and Williams—although both campaign organizations were clearly preoccupied with the problem, and certain supporters of both candidates sought, for a variety of reasons, specifically to make sex the issue.

One typical reaction to women candidates, especially in a place as preoccupied as America with the symbol of equality, is the assertion that "sex doesn't make any difference to me. I'm looking for the best person for the job." But as human beings, we see much of what we see about one another through the prisms of gender (see Deaux and Major 1987; for classic psychological theory of the effects of gendered expectations in even the simplest social interactions, see Deaux and Major 1990, and see Lucchesi and Edwards 1993, for an attempt to develop such a psychological framework for the study of political leadership). Public women—even such notorious "honorary men" as Margaret Thatcher—are never *not* seen to be the physical, biological women they are, although just what that may mean varies enormously from perceiver to perceiver, since the prisms of gender through which perceptions are refracted also vary (Sapiro 1993).

As we have already suggested, some of the most intricate facets of the prism have to do with leadership, how it looks, how it behaves. Political women (but not, until very recently, political men) have had to walk a careful line: they must present themselves as at least "feminine" enough not to raise any fears that they are not "womanly," but at the same time, they cannot be too *stereotypically* feminine or they will not appear to be strong enough to lead. (Men, in the past, have not been expected to demonstrate any "feminine" characteristics of nurturance and the like, although that may be changing.) Women must, in short, offer a harmonious blend of androgynous characteristics, regardless of the office they seek, but especially when they are seeking political chief executive positions (Pierce 1989; Huddy and Terkildsen 1993, 1993a). It was not especially difficult for the Richards campaign to portray Ann Richards in this androgynous light; it did not require any particular distortion of her genuine personality to present her as "tough" (she is) and yet "caring" (again, she is).

It was maintaining this androgynous portrayal, however, that sometimes required contrivances—presentations of Richards out hunting pheasant to show how close she was to the Texas "Good Ol' Boy" image, for example, or, when the campaign had reached new lows of bitterness, an advertisement showing Richards strolling arm-in-arm with her elderly father, at least partly to demonstrate that she had been born into a real family, that she *had* had normal parents, just like anyone else. Clayton Williams' handlers also, though less often, tried to show his "feminine" side, surrounding him with small children or adolescents, but his image was always less differentiated than that of Richards (just as his actual personality seems genuinely less multifaceted than does hers). In any case, the particular emphasis was never (for obvious reasons) on the fact that Williams was a *man* running for Governor, but was instead on the fact that Richards was a *woman* doing so. When she won, she became a "woman Governor," a symbolic woman.

The primary and general election campaigns, and Governor Richards' activities in the first years of her administration, then, give us the opportunity to plumb a number of questions: How do women reach high political office? Once they are there, what do women do that might differ from what men do? What is the weight of differing expectations that "symbolic women" bear? How will women's increased presence in political leadership positions change our conceptions of political leadership—or, indeed, *will* it?

In these pages, we examine these questions by fitting

them into the large, textured tapestries of gender politics and the white-hot crucible of Texas politics. But, because Ann Richards' victory did not arise de novo, we begin by examining women, gender, and politics in the twentieth century in Texas, by focusing on turn-of-the-century suffrage efforts and the first woman to be elected Governor of Texas, Miriam "Ma" Ferguson. Nor does the story end when the last ballot is counted, for just as everyone speculated about the woman candidate, so they were also speculating about the woman Governor, and about the sort of leadership she would provide. We offer our comments and judgments on that question in the epilogue.

Almost sixty years passed from the end of Governor Ma Ferguson's tenure to the commencement of that of Governor Ann Richards. Between the two, one other woman had arisen to challenge preconceptions about women in politics. Frances "Sissy" Farenthold, a reform, progressive Democrat who first entered the Texas House of Representatives in 1968 (and whose name was placed in nomination for Vice-President at the 1972 Democratic National Nominating Convention), made two brave but unsuccessful attempts to capture the Democratic nomination for Governor, once in 1972 and again in 1974. She had, early in her tenure in the Texas House, become the "unofficial den mother of a pack of reform warriors soon dubbed 'The Dirty Thirty'" (Lasher and Bentley 1980: 45), and her aggressive reform activities were not welcomed by the political establishment. She was equally aggressive about women and politics, and about her own feminism (Weddington, Hickie, and Fitzgerald 1977), and the Texas political culture was simply not ready to accommodate the challenge that she posed to it. Sissy Farenthold may have helped to prepare the ground for Ann Richards, but it would not be fertile enough for planting for almost another two decades.

In that same period, Richards' own education as a public woman took place. It culminated in the development of Richards' gubernatorial campaign, the unfolding of events in it, and, at last, the voters' choice. We have devoted our attention to each of these parts of the story in turn, beginning with Miriam Ferguson and her opponents, the feminists of the "Petticoat Lobby."

"T. H., I may run my head off and then get thrown out of the race," Ferguson said. "What do you think about running through my wife if that happens?" "Well," answered McGregor, "if a man can run a grocery store in his wife's name, I don't see why he couldn't run a state that way." "By gosh, I believe I'll try it," Jim declared.

—JIM FERGUSON, 1924 (recounted in Brown 1984: 217)

Ann uses her charm . . . but of course, when she's tough, it's endearing too . . . She's made it easier for every woman who comes after . . . Every schoolgirl in Texas can dream now. Used to be, when I was growing up in East Texas, the only role models were Ma Ferguson and the Kilgore Rangerettes. Now there's another.

—MOLLY IVINS, interview with the authors, 14 May 1991
(for information on this and all the interviews we conducted, see Appendix A)

Gender and Texas Political Culture in the Twentieth Century

Texas, one of the most populous and economically significant of the American states, is also the manufactory of legend: the cowboy on the Chisholm Trail, the Alamo, the gushers in the Permian Basin that bathed the world in oil. In politics, too, Texas has contributed its vivid share: Sam Rayburn (U.S. House Speaker), Lyndon Baines Johnson . . . even George Bush wishes to lay claim to the Texas mystique. Its political culture, denoted "moralist/traditionalist" in an Elazarian formulation, has been an often bewildering collection of deep conservatism, populism, and hostility to government intervention in its rowdy economy. But for all its people's suspicion of government, Texas can surprise observers. It was the first southern state to ratify the Nineteenth Amendment, in 1919, after granting women the right to vote in state party primaries the previous year. It ratified the Equal Rights Amendment in 1972. A Texas Federal District Judge, Sarah Hughes, is the only woman ever to have administered the oath of office to an American President (Lyndon Baines Johnson, following John F. Kennedy's assassination in Dallas; see Crawford and Ragsdale 1982). In 1924, James E. Ferguson having seven years earlier become the only Texas Governor ever to be impeached, his wife, Miriam Amanda Wallace ("Ma") Ferguson, could lay a claim to being the first American woman elected Governor "in her own right" (even if she might have to share the honor with Democrat Nellie Tayloe Ross of Wyoming, who was also sworn in as Governor in 1925). Ross, too, succeeded a husband, albeit one who had died in office rather than one who had been cast out of it.

(Matthews [1992] calls Ross the "first woman" but does not mention Ferguson; Texas sources, understandably, claim the "first" for Ferguson but do not mention Ross.) As the chapter epigraphs above and the following pages make clear, however, Ma Ferguson's election was not a triumph for women's integration into politics.

TWO GOVERNORS

Ma, and even more so her husband, "Farmer Jim" Ferguson, are examples of the almost mythical colorful personalities who have dominated Texas politics. On 6 November 1990, voters chose between two candidates amply suited to continue the tradition of Texas political drama. Their choice, by a narrow margin, was Ann Richards. Her defeat of Clayton Williams, a businessman and rancher who gained extraordinary attention for his gaffes during the campaign, came only after voters had wearied of months of rancor in both party primaries, followed by a general election campaign in which issues, as well as qualities of leadership, were often lost in the hubbub of insults, unsubstantiated charges, and barefisted campaign advertising. While most observers agree that Richards' survival of the particularly bitter Democratic primary and runoff showed both her and the voters that she could pass through one of the most searing political crucibles in the nation, her success was never certain or even thought likely until the ballots were counted.

Richards' ability to survive a grueling campaign was an issue because she is a woman. Voters do not reward any candidate perceived as weak, regardless of sex. But strength and toughness are not stereotypically feminine traits, and voters also eschew candidates who depart too far from widely shared norms of behavior and presentation of self for their sex. Richards was thus faced with the need to present a delicate balance of the warmth, compassion, and accountability for which women in office have been praised in the last decade, and the steely strength Texans have always expected of their leaders.

Ann Richards did not arise de novo, of course. She was born and raised in the midst of Texas culture; indeed, her childhood was contemporaneous with the twilight of "Fergusonism" in Texas politics. Her mother-in-law, an important influence on Ann the young woman, had been a particularly striking example of the strain of Texas activist women who had won the suffrage for themselves, only to use it for progressive and community causes. But there are other parallels between the 1920s and the 1990s in Texas: in both eras, considerable ferment over feminism and gender roles spilled colorfully into politics. And the earlier period has left a legacy for our own. It is useful, then, to turn our gaze back to the early part of the century (and one additional benefit is that some wonderful stories emerge there, too).

Before World War II, Texas politics was dominated as much by personalities as it was by issues. Because it was an adamantly one-party system, with the only meaningful competition for office taking place in the Democratic primaries and runoff primaries, personality cults and special-interest factions—also frequently manifested in the personalities of their leaders—were the red meat and drink of electoral conflict. With few exceptions, campaigns were unrelievedly ad hominem, as scathing, if not more so, than anything seen in the "negative" campaigning of the 1980s and 1990s. The dominant political issues centered on a kind of agrarian populism, prohibition, a pale reflection of the national progressive agenda, and the Ku Klux Klan. "Farmer Jim" Ferguson turned this often unsavory version of personality politics and frequently inflammatory issues to extraordinary advantage, maintaining his position as the "most important figure in Texas politics from 1914 to 1934" (Brown 1984: 4), "distract[ing] the voter's attention from other matters and caus[ing] him to think of politics in terms of his like or dislike for 'Farmer Jim.' 'Ferguson men' swore by Old Jim" (Key 1949: 265).

Building his base among poor white tenant farmers—the "boys at the forks of the creek," as he fondly called them—as well as among ethnic Germans and liquor and brewing interests, he won the 1914 gubernatorial election, and in his first term did act on some of his populist campaign promises. Upon reelection in 1916 (Texas Governors served two-year terms until the mid-1970s), however, he revealed the propensities for dispensing patronage, accumulating money, and amassing self-aggrandizement that were to be his only notable characteristics for the rest of his political career. Progressives and prohibitionists, as well as the old Texas elite, had despised him from the beginning. They did not fail to take their opportunity to act against him after he began meddling with the University of Texas early in his second term. He demanded that several professors be fired and, when the University defied him, he vetoed its entire fiscal appropriation for the coming year. This was too much, and all of his opponents arrayed their forces against him.

The Texas House of Representatives passed twenty-one articles of impeachment against Ferguson, and the Texas Senate found him guilty of ten. He resigned his office the day before the Senate completed its proceedings against him, in the hope that he might sidestep the permanent ban from holding office constitutionally levied upon anyone impeached. Although he tried to run for Governor in 1918, and tried to run for the U.S. Senate in his wife's name in 1922 (despite his later claims that he had only thought of doing such a thing in 1924), he was subsequently prevented by the state Democratic Party Executive Committee from placing his name on a ballot (Brown 1984; Anderson, Murray, and Farley 1989). His ambition and his desire for power seem to have been insatiable: he never consulted his wife Miriam before he placed her name in nomination for the Democratic gubernatorial primary of 1924, and he continued this ploy in every election but one for the next sixteen years.

From the impeachment of "Farmer Jim" in 1917 to Ma Ferguson's election in 1924, however, a revolution in women's status occurred. Women achieved the suffrage, and suffragists, now staunch political activists, found themselves in horrified opposition to a woman Governor.

GENDER ROLES AND PROGRESSIVISM
AT THE TURN OF THE CENTURY

The settlement of a frontier requires women, or so we have always believed. In order to colonize North America, the London Company, Lords Baltimore and Southampton and others, and the British government itself all launched overt strategies to induce women to emigrate. Single women, for example, were offered money and title to land *providing that,* shortly after arriving in the New World, they married (when, of course, ownership of the money and land would shift to their husbands). Only this could "make the men more setled and lesse moveable who by defect thereof (as is credibly reported) stay there but to gett some thing and then return for England" (quoted in Spruill [1938] 1972: 8). In short, only wives (with the children and attachments that they bring) could transform an outpost into a secure community. As Americans moved westward, that same assumption about the civilizing influence of women held sway.

Early in the nineteenth century, the settling of the Texas frontier produced stories of incredible hardship. But as the nineteenth century waned, the "land that was 'fine for men and horses' but 'hell on women and oxen' was changing . . ." (Lasher and Bentley 1980: xvii), and by the end of the century, women all over Texas had succeeded not only in building stable communities, but in organizing themselves as well— into literary societies, study groups, and other self-improvement organizations. More important to the future of women in Texas politics, though, was that countless women organized themselves into community volunteer societies dedicated to improving the plight of the elderly and indigent and the working conditions of women and children. By doing so, these Texas women were creating their own political apprenticeship opportunities. They were making claims on the public sphere on behalf of "traditional (private) women's" concerns, demanding that the polis aid women in caring (if not in providing) for their families (see Sapiro 1986 on gender at the birth of the welfare state). In so doing, they were also learning how political systems function, and how to "do politics." And as was true of women nationwide, they became the rank and file of the woman suffrage movement, just as they were already the soldiers in the Progressive war on social ills (see Scott 1984 on women's transformation from voluntarism to political activism at the turn of the century, and Cott 1987 on skilled advocacy by women's organizations of social welfare concerns both before and after suffrage). Woman suffrage and progressive social welfare policies were closely, almost naturally, linked in the overarching political orientations of these women. They saw women's roles as those of the makers and preservers of their communities. The suffrage—the chance to act as citizens—was to them an essential facilitator of those roles. In many ways, these women were making exactly the arguments that many feminists make today: women must be a part of politics, the argument goes, because they will bring a new compassion, accountability, and responsiveness to the political arena.

In Texas, though, the growth of the woman suffrage movement was slower and more uneven than it was elsewhere, particularly in the north. Occasional references to woman suffrage—including even, for the first time, in state constitutional conventions—were heard in the 1860s and 1870s, but little grass-roots organization occurred (Taylor 1987). The Women's Christian Temperance Union was the first statewide organization to endorse woman suffrage, in the 1880s (Lasher and Bentley 1980: xvii). But organizations devoted *explicitly* to the suffrage struggle could not sustain themselves until the new century. Geographic distances, the difficulty of communications, a fair measure of opprobrium, the confusion of the woman suffrage question with questions of "negro" and alien suffrage—all gave the drive toward suffrage a fit-and-start quality (Taylor 1987: 18–23), unlike its more consistent momentum in upper midwestern and northeastern states (Flexner 1973). Texas suffragists also differed with the national movement in the nineteenth century: some believed that suffrage work should be carried on by Texas women, not by "outsiders," and conflict over a proposed visit to Texas by Susan B. Anthony cleaved the only statewide organization, leaving it, in 1894 and 1895, with two contending and opposed "presidents" (one for, the other against Anthony). But by 1913, a Texas affiliate of the National American Woman Suffrage Association was beginning to flourish, and national leader Carrie Chapman Catt could be received in Texas warmly, without exciting the controversy that Susan B. Anthony had attracted two decades earlier. And in 1916, a much smaller Texas affiliate of Alice Paul's militant National Woman's Party was established. So, as World War I approached, both strains of the national suffrage movement were present in Texas, although the Texas political system, perpetually conservative, found the more conventional Texas Woman's Suffrage Association (the Texas Equal Suffrage Association after 1916) more acceptable. And it was from this group that feminist activities in the immediate postsuffrage period would spring (Taylor 1987: 23–33).

Annette, Elizabeth, and Katherine Finnigan, Houstonian sisters, are credited with having revived the movement after the turn of the century. Although their efforts to organize the state were not successful, and they eventually left Texas, enough women remained active—particularly in Austin—that by 1912, a genuine (if exceptionally thinly spread) statewide woman-suffrage network could form, and the pace of progress toward suffrage began to pick up. A woman-suffrage resolution failed by only four votes to gain the two-thirds needed to emerge from the Texas House in 1915, and a similar resolution in 1917 also narrowly failed. But also in 1917, "Farmer Jim" Ferguson—whom suffrage activist Jane Yelvington McCallum (known as "Jane Y") called the "implacable foe of woman suffrage and of every great moral issue for which women stood" (Taylor 1987: 37)—was impeached, and the savvy suffragettes seized their main chance.

The Texas woman suffrage movement had been one of the most vigorous groups in its opposition to Ferguson, and one of the most energetic in working for his impeachment. Progressives, prohibitionists, and supporters of President Woodrow Wilson were largely in favor of the vote for women; they were also vehemently anti-Ferguson, and were thus the natural allies of the feminists, whose capable leaders (such as McCallum) were making women a genuine power in Texas Democratic politics even without the vote. Anti-Ferguson forces in the state legislature welcomed the women's efforts in the impeachment struggle (Crawford and Ragsdale 1982: 225). Upon Ferguson's ignominious departure from office, women found a staunch comrade in the person of William P. Hobby, who, as Lieutenant Governor, had succeeded "Farmer Jim."

Hobby called a special legislative session in March 1918, to consider granting women suffrage in the all-important Democratic party primary. Primary suffrage could be achieved by mere legislative act, requiring only a simple majority rather than the two-thirds majority required for full suffrage (Taylor 1987: 37). Once the legislature passed the bill, suffragettes worked furiously to get women registered in the seventeen days remaining before the 1918 Democratic primary would be held, and distributed almost half a million sample ballots to newly enfranchised women, to help them familiarize themselves with this new process they were now a part of. Suffragettes also repaid Hobby with vigorous efforts on behalf of his campaign. Hobby was elected Governor in his own right, and the feminist Annie Webb Blanton was also elected State Superintendent of Public Instruction (Taylor 1987: 37–38).

In 1919, with Hobby's full support, a resolution providing for the complete enfranchisement of women emerged from the Texas legislature and was to be put before the voters. The suffragettes engaged in an enormous mass campaign for passage of the resolution (antisuffragists were also active, but largely through the distribution of literature rather than in grass-roots organizations). Oddly, though, the woman-suffrage resolution was doomed by another Progressive reform: woman suffrage was included with alien *disenfranchisement* (reformers believed that disenfranchisement of noncitizens would help stem political corruption), and a vote for or against one was a vote for or against the other. Since the referendum was offered on a general election ballot, women could not vote on it—but aliens could. The woman-suffrage resolution was defeated by 25,000 votes. Some tried to argue that the result was actually a mandate against woman suffrage, and others even went so far as to demand that women's primary suffrage be retracted (Taylor 1987: 39, 40, 46).

The now thoroughly skilled feminists barely paused to draw breath before turning their attention to the *federal* suffrage amendment, released to the states for approval less than a month after the Texas referendum had failed. Suffragists claimed that the state was still bound to them by the woman-suffrage plank in the Democratic platform. Governor Hobby, keeping faith with them, called the legislature into special session to consider the federal amendment on 23 June 1919. On 28 June, Texas became the ninth state, and the first in the South, to have ratified the Nineteenth Amendment to the U.S. Constitution, and Texas women were "citizens at last" (Taylor 1987: 46).

"A BONNET OR A HOOD": MA FERGUSON AND GENDER IN TEXAS POLITICS

By 1924, with full suffrage rights established, a coalition of women's organizations, composed of women whose apprenticeship in the suffrage and Progressive movements had made them highly skilled political activists, formed the Women's Joint Legislative Council (which we shall examine more closely in the next section of this chapter). Designed to serve as a kind of peak association of women's groups, parallel to such peak associations on the national level as the Women's Joint Congressional Committee or the Women's Joint Legislative Conference, to promote social welfare and antidiscrimination bills, the Women's Joint Legislative Council was dubbed the "Petticoat Lobby" by patronizing legislators. Its amused leader "Jane Y" McCallum turned the name to the group's advantage, and the Petticoat Lobby became one of the most successful lobbies in Texas history, seeing a mass of educational and welfare policy through the legislative maze for the next decade or so (Brown 1984; Anderson et al. 1989; Crawford and Ragsdale 1982).

In that same year, though, McCallum and the Petticoat

Lobby faced a dilemma. From a confusing field (including two candidates named Davidson, the first Democratic gubernatorial primary produced two candidates: Judge Felix Robertson and Miriam Ferguson. This put the Petticoat Lobby and all other progressive groups in the position of having to choose between the Ku Klux Klan, for whom Robertson was to be the long-awaited passport to the Governor's Mansion, or "Farmer Jim," violently anti-Klan but a "wet," the former enemy of the vote for women, impeached and disgraced, and now running in his wife's name. "If I am elected I am going to be Governor," Mrs. Ferguson had said, but "The vote by which I am now leading, though the governorship may not be my portion, has vindicated my Jim, my big, fine Jim, and has in part removed the stigma of the blow that swept us from the gubernatorial mansion in 1917" (Brown 1984: 225).

The latter portion of Mrs. Ferguson's statement is the more revealing. She allowed herself to be photographed (and in one case was posed in an old, borrowed sunbonnet, giving rise to the "bonnet or [Klan] hood" campaign theme), and made a few faint remarks at campaign rallies. It was nonetheless clear to all who the Governor would be. "Two governors for the price of one!" was an unabashed campaign slogan, as was "Me for Ma . . . and I ain't got a dern thing against Pa!" What could feminist women and progressive men do? The victor of the second (runoff) primary would certainly be the next Governor (although, in the event, the Republican candidate in the general election received a historically large number of votes). Ferguson's opposition to the Klan was merely opposition to its power: on the campaign trail, he was vigorously white supremacist and anti-Semitic. But others' hatred of the Klan gave the Fergusons their chance; anti-Ferguson forces, including the Petticoat Lobby, confronted with the "evil of two lessers," chose the lesser of two evils, and made Miriam Ferguson the first American woman Governor, albeit in name only.

Ma wore an elegant black satin gown trimmed in chinchilla to take her oath of office—contrary to the voters' image of her, she was of affluent background and had a college education (Crawford and Ragsdale 1982: 203–218; Weddington, Hickie, and Fitzgerald 1977). Jim moved his desk into the Governor's office.

Before her first term was completed, charges of corruption were again thick in the air, while no substantial legislative goals were accomplished. Ma, indeed, seemed most concerned about securing legislation overturning Jim's impeachment (she was unsuccessful) and with pardoning a variety of convicted individuals, many of whom had been supporters of Jim. Cries for *her* impeachment were subdued by the fear that Jim had "already turned one impeachment to his advantage" and by claims, especially by feminists, that she was the dupe of her husband (Brown 1984: 294). And many Texans were becoming embarrassed by the amount of national attention (or infamy) that the Fergusons had brought the state.

T. R. Fehrenbach, author of what was for years one of the standard histories of Texas (a history that strikes us most now for its failure even once to mention woman suffrage, the Petticoat Lobby, or indeed any activities of women in politics at all), offers an impression of other, less condemnatory reactions to Ma:

> *Ma Ferguson provided the color the Ferguson type sought and had to have. She was news, merely by being in office. But Ferguson himself was the governor of Texas, in everything but name. He was appointed to the powerful highway commission, which let juicy contracts; he dominated the executive office from the bedroom. All this provoked criticism in responsible quarters, but in others it provided Texas with endless fun. It took the mind of the common man off his troubles. No small portion of Ma Ferguson's support came from people who consciously or unconsciously believed in cutting "the powers" down to size. Ma Ferguson, and her husband, focused much resentment among those people who equated commonalty [sic] with real democracy and professed to see social value in being "common as an old shoe." (Fehrenbach 1968: 646–647)*

Fehrenbach's amused contempt for this reversal of "normal" boudoir leadership—he calls Miriam's *first* administration the *"second* Ferguson administration" (p. 647, emphasis added)—is obvious, as is his disregard of women's genuine political activity in the period. But it must be said that, even in retrospect, some elements of Ma's tenure as Governor can only be seen as sheer Texas political fun; two apocryphal stories emerging from her first term make this clear. One tale has it that, upon being approached about supporting bilingual language programs in Texas schools, Ma replied, "If English was good enough for Jesus Christ, it's good enough for the school children of Texas!" Another, with sly reference to her propensity to grant executive clemency to virtually anyone for whom her husband sought it, spins the yarn of a man who, in the State House elevator, accidentally brushes against Ma. He politely says, "Pardon me, Governor." She responds, "Oh, you'll have to see Jim about that."[1]

Miriam was unquestionably manipulated by Jim, but she cannot have been entirely the innocent dupe, the "slave wife," that the Petticoat Lobby said she was. An early opponent of suffrage, she disingenuously tried to co-opt women's rights in her campaigns. She appointed the first woman ever to hold the office of Secretary of State, but she also opposed Texas' participation in the federal Sheppard-Towner maternal health-care program and opposed the federal child-labor amendment, both very dear to the Petticoat Lobby's hearts (Brown 1984: 257, 260, 488). She ran for reelection in 1926 but lost to Dan Moody, the progressive Attorney General who served during her first questionable administration, and who benefited from the energetic support of the Petticoat Lobby.

Miriam Ferguson entered the Governor's Mansion again in 1933, having won the election of 1932, and if her second and final term was not marked by any particular accomplishment, neither was it tainted by the scandals of the Fergusons' earlier administrations (Anderson et al. 1989: 159–161). In 1940, when the Fergusons tried one last time to offer Texans "two governors for the price of one," Ma placed fourth in the Democratic primary, and Fergusonism appeared finally to have passed from the scene (Brown 1984: 433–434). Some argue that, through the last years of her life, Ma Ferguson matured politically, eventually becoming a strong supporter of and even campaigner for Lyndon Baines Johnson (Weddington, Hickie, and Fitzgerald 1977).

But no matter how much contemporary feminists might wish to point to Texas' first woman Governor and her "accomplishments," even in simple virtual-representation terms, she simply cannot be thought of as a model of challenge to traditional gender-role stereotypes. On the other hand, the women of the Petticoat Lobby provide an important stream of historical continuity in Texas women's political activism. Ann Richards would no doubt have liked and greatly admired "Jane Y" McCallum, or Minnie Fisher Cunningham—who herself ran for Governor in 1944 after having run for the U.S. Senate in 1928 (Taylor 1987: 8)—and Richards has surely shared many of the political values of such women. The Petticoat Lobby saw itself, and not Miriam Ferguson, as the "real" representative of women and women's concerns in Texas and national politics. Whichever way the representational argument might be settled, certainly the Petticoat Lobby became an estimable political force.

THE "PETTICOAT LOBBY": WOMEN'S POLITICAL ACTIVISM IN THE 1920S AND 1930S

After the achievement of suffrage in 1920, women's political activity, at least as manifested in the energies of the former suffragettes, redoubled. They had spent 1919 in a whirlwind of education programs, teaching newly enfranchised women how to use their votes. They contributed in 1920 to the election of Pat Neff, a pro-suffrage Progressive, as Governor, and to the election of the feminist educator Annie Webb Blanton as the State Superintendent of Public Instruction (Crawford and Ragsdale 1982), and they assisted in Neff's reelection in 1922. By the beginning of the legislative session in January of 1923, the Women's Joint Legislative Council—the Petticoat Lobby—was ready to present its first carefully developed policy program (about which more is discussed below) before the legislature, and it advocated an even more ambitious program in the 1925 session (also Miriam Ferguson's first term as Governor).

A curious set of events made Governor Neff responsible, before he left office, for another "first" in the history of women in Texas politics: the creation of a temporary "Petticoat Supreme Court." A case concerning a fraternal organization, the Woodmen of the World, proved to be a conundrum for the Governor, since the three sitting Supreme Court Justices as well as most qualified men who might have replaced them, were all also members of the organization. Governor Neff finally solved his problem of vested interest on the bench by appointing to it three women: Hattie Henenberg and Ruth Brazzil, as associate justices, and Hortense Ward, as chief justice. The women sat from January to May of 1925, dispensed with the Woodmen case, were "commended for the brevity of their opinions, and left the bench. For a brief period of their history, Texans had a woman governor and an all-female state supreme court at the same time" (Lasher and Bentley 1980: xviii).

This oddity, as colorful as it is, also merits our consideration because of the neatness with which it raises questions about gender roles and politics. Specifically, it reveals the way much of the *same* constellation of traditional gender roles produces both apolitical *and* political women, but produces gendered institutions as well. That is to say, sex and gender have consequences beyond those we most readily see, at both the individual level (Is politics women's place?) and the level of the political system (Are institutions built for men rather than women? How do women get into them, and how do they change them once they are there?).

We would call Miriam Ferguson and the "Petticoat Supreme Court" (while we wonder whether one cannot weary of the term "petticoat") examples of *apolitical* women. How can we call them apolitical? We can because they are, essentially, no more than replacements or stand-ins for men, and they are available to play such roles only because they have *not*, indeed, been (or been seen as) legitimate actors in the political system. Politically experienced and effective feminists such as "Jane Y" McCallum or Minnie Fisher

Cunningham, after all, were not invited to sit on the Petticoat Supreme Court. Because, the gendered aphorism would have it, politics is dirty, no place for a woman, then women are not tarnished: recall that no qualified men could be found to fill the supreme court bench and, thus, female replacements had to be resorted to. Even in Ma Ferguson's case, though many might well have felt that she was entirely complicit in Jim's venalities, the gendered division of men in the public sphere and women in the private sphere meant that Ma *could not* officially be held accountable for Jim. Thus, paradoxically, she could become his stand-in. Of course, if women are so removed from the political system that they can be unsullied, temporary, "honorary men" in certain extraordinary circumstances, that also means that in *ordinary* circumstances they have neither much political power nor many legitimate political roles beyond, as in this case, the right to vote.

Consider, on the other hand, "traditional" gender role socialization's production of *political* women, such as the women of the Petticoat Lobby. These women were not trying to be like men, much less to be stand-ins or replacements for men. The Petticoat Lobby activists were highly conscious of their distinct gender roles, and of differences between those roles and the roles of men. Indeed, they were steeped in the "difference" perspective on women's unique contribution to the political arena that influenced feminism so much during the fin de siècle and the early twentieth century (see Cott 1987; 1990). Far from trying to be political men, they were instead exerting a distinctively "womanly" political role. They believed, as we have already argued, that women could—*must*—represent substantively different issues from those represented in status-quo politics (see Tolleson Rinehart 1992 for additional considerations of this point). At the same time that they meant to be vigorous policy advocates, however, they also intended that their political behavior, as well as their beliefs, would remain "feminine."

In her own words, "Jane Y" McCallum makes these emphases vividly evident, and so we will quote at length from her own assessment of the Petticoat Lobby's successes in the 1920s:

> *The desire of the women to concentrate their efforts*
> *on a few fundamental, well understood measures*
> *was made possible of fulfillment because of the*
> *overlapping interests of the several organizations [in*
> *the Women's Joint Legislative Council]. Only six*
> *proposed measures appeared on the official program*
> *that each of the 181 lawmakers found spread on top*
> *of his desk on the day of his arrival at the Capitol*
> *January, 1923 . . . And acceptance of the Federal*
> *Sheppard-Towner [maternal and infant health-care]*
> *Act, appeared among the first measures on the*
> *women's program. Furthermore, the "Petticoat*
> *Lobbyists," as the women workers were calmly*
> *dubbed, had calmly circulated a "talking point"*
> *calling attention to their state's inconsistency in*
> *Federal matters and concluding with the declara-*
> *tion that "a state bending every effort to secure all*
> *Federal Aid possible for the highways, and accept-*
> *ing Federal Aid on the 50-50 plan to promote agri-*
> *cultural interest, should not hesitate to accept*
> *Federal Aid on the same 50-50 plan to promote the*
> *health and security of its mothers and babies . . .*
> *[Gradually full realization dawned as opposition to*
> *the Petticoat Lobby's program began to falter]: Each*
> *member [of the legislature] had groups, scores, scads*
> *of women among his constituents who were intelli-*
> *gently informed and actively interested in all of the*
> *measures advocated by their representatives, the*
> *petticoat lobby . . . Furthermore, the lobbyists*
> *seemed to be schooled against argumentative,*
> *militant or any except "lady like," and elusively*
> *intelligent tactics . . . [After one senator had made a*
> *blustering speech against their issues, he said,]*
> *"Why, they complimented my speech and said they*
> *wanted me to make one equally good, but on their*
> *side, next time. I tell you, you can't down them."*
> *(Reproduced in Taylor 1987: 222, 224)*

The women were clever, passionately committed to what they believed to be (and indeed was) a truly different substantive policy agenda, and completely comfortable advocating this agenda within the confines of behavior that was traditionally "lady like" (see also Andersen 1990, for a general picture of women's activism in the 1920s). While the only *superficially* untraditional aspect of their behavior was that it was occurring inside the halls of the legislature, in fact what they intended to accomplish was virtually revolutionary. And their preparation and tactics paid off: in 1923, all six of their bills passed the legislature and were signed into law by Governor Neff. In 1925, seven of their ten legislative proposals emerged from the legislature, although, as McCallum says, "one bill was vetoed by the new governor [Miriam Ferguson, whom she no doubt intentionally refuses to name], and another mutilated" (Taylor 1987: 225–226).

The Petticoat Lobby did not have to suffer for long the irritating thorn in the side that Miriam Ferguson was to them. They threw themselves into the 1926 election, pointedly campaigning for Dan Moody, claiming that Ma was not the choice of the women of Texas (Crawford and Ragsdale 1982: 229; Brown 1984: 306–307). Moody, in victory, named McCallum his Secretary of State, and she continued in that office under Governor Ross Sterling.

When Ma entered the gubernatorial election of 1932, again fronting for Jim, McCallum said, "Mrs. Ferguson never has and never can cause [the women of Texas] aught but shame and humiliation" (Crawford and Ragsdale 1982: 230). But although, to the Petticoat Lobby's dismay, Ma won, other women had moved into public office as well, and they and the Petticoat Lobby continued to make their influence felt through the 1930s. In fact, they remained effective about a decade longer than did the national peak associations—the Women's Joint Congressional Committee and the Women's Joint Legislative Council, neither of which survived the onset of the Great Depression (Flexner 1973; Buechler 1990; Matthews 1992; Wiesen Cook 1992). It is tantalizing to ask whether there was much interaction between the Texas and national groups. They were composed of representatives from similar organizations, such as the League of Women Voters (for which Texas' Minnie Fisher Cunningham served as national Executive Secretary during the 1920s), even though the Women's Joint Legislative Council also included groups from further left on the political spectrum, such as the Women's Trade Union League and the Consumer's League (Wiesen Cook 1992: 321), that would be especially controversial in conservative, anti-union Texas. And they supported the same progressive social legislation, including proposals such as the Sheppard-Towner Maternity and Infant Protection Act and its state-level equivalents. The unfortunately small amount of extant research on these groups at either national or state level makes it impossible for us to do more than speculate. The Petticoat Lobby probably did have considerable contact with its national counterparts; it was too efficiently organized and too effective not to have been conversant with actors on the national scene. But it may also be that the Petticoat Lobby did not advertise its national connections, if it had them, since its effectiveness lay in its ladylike "acceptability" and its members' unquestionable standing among substantial Texas families. On account of both the idea that only "real Texans" can play in Texas politics (still true today) and the necessity for the appearance of moderate reasonableness, the Petticoat Lobby may not have wished to emphasize that its agenda was shared by groups on the political left or from alien places such as New York and Massachusetts. If this strategy of downplaying its connection to groups outside Texas was in fact adopted, it might also explain why the Petticoat Lobby remained effective for a decade longer than did the national groups, who were seeing their effectiveness reduced as early as the mid-1920s (Matthews 1992: 183). But whether it was the case that this strategy was adopted or not, the Texas feminists of the suffrage and immediate post-suffrage period were not, by and large, to have the kind of national visibility that some Texas women would have in the feminist renascence of the 1960s and 1970s, when Liz Carpenter served as Lyndon Baines Johnson's press secretary, Frances "Sissy" Farenthold's name was placed in nomination to be the vice-presidential candidate of the Democratic party, Sarah Weddington was to argue *Roe v. Wade* before the United States Supreme Court, and Barbara Jordan was to become the symbolic conscience of the nation in the U.S. House Watergate hearings—and even these women had a greater impact on the national scene than they did in Texas. After the suffragists' time had passed, and before the latter women's time had come, however, women's political presence in Texas receded into the background, as it did in much of the nation.

PROGRESSIVISM SUCCUMBS TO CONSERVATISM

The advent of World War II gave women another set of invigorating roles to play, and women in Texas were not behindhand in their efforts. The end of the war, and the onset of 1950s popular culture, though, severely diminished an organized women's political presence. Affluent, educated white women could be and were heard from in those groups, such as the League of Women Voters, that were the inheritors of the suffrage movement (Ware 1990). Women of color raised their voices in the great movement for civil rights (unfortunately, deliberate and unconscious racism kept white women and women of color largely divided from one another in their political efforts as in their day-to-day lives, even in such purportedly enlightened and egalitarian groups as the League). But in Texas, as elsewhere, women (especially white, middle-class women) were bombarded with cultural sanctions against anything but aspirations to the role of perfect wife and mother. Even the proportion of women who attended institutions of higher education fell to levels that were below those of the 1930s and that were not to rebound until the 1980s (Solomon 1984; Tolleson Rinehart 1992).

It can be argued that the "difference" orientation of suffrage and social feminists in the nineteenth and early twentieth centuries hampered the thorough integration of women into politics; women argued, rightly, that the expertise emerging from their "special sphere" (that of the private, domestic domain, of care and nurturance, and of the preservation of the community) uniquely prepared them to cope with crises such as nursing and public health in the Civil War, or the tremendous social and domestic dislocations of the Great

Depression. But the problem here is that of the very unique-
ness on which women's claims were based. Their political
activity was based not on some broad, well-accepted acknowledgment of women's full citizenship, but rather on women's
"difference." And once these new policy questions, where
formerly there had been no turf for men to defend, took a
permanent place on the public agenda (public health after
the Civil War, social policy during the Depression), male
bureaucrats and elected officials predictably seized political
control (see the discussion in Matthews 1992: 186–188; see
also Sapiro 1986; Tolleson Rinehart 1987). Even women's
activities in World War II were treated as unique or special,
and not as the "normal" activities of citizens—as postwar
pop-Freudian propaganda, intended to drive women back into
the home, makes clear. With no thoroughgoing mass
resocialization of attitudes toward women's place in the polis,
it is not surprising, no matter how regrettable, that the political energies of women in the 1920s and 1930s dwindled to
the "doldrums" of the 1950s and early 1960s. If anything,
women's doldrums were deeper in Texas than they were elsewhere (see Davidson 1990: 162–164, 166 on women in the
Democratic party at this time).

Ann Richards, coming to young adulthood in this low
period, was also influenced by the culture's demand for perfect wifedom and motherhood. But there had been other in-
fluences in her life, too: her mother had insistently tried to
prepare her for a broad citizen role, and her mother-in-law,
Eleanor Richards, a sophisticated, interested, and interesting
woman, had been a founder of the League of Women Voters
in Waco, Texas (Richards 1989). These influential women,
and Richards' own inchoate sense of social justice, led her to
an early condemnation of what Texas politics had become.
After the headiness of pre–World War II progressivism, Texas
politics in the postwar period reverted to recalcitrant conservatism, shaped by racism, oil, and big money, with very little
room for more than a tiny number of women (such as stead-
fast Democrats Billie Carr and "Frankie" Rudolph) to play
significant political roles. Richards could do nothing but engage with the political system, first on the question of racial

justice. But by the 1970s, her questions about women led Richards *herself* to participate in the rediscovery of the history of women in Texas politics. Some of the results of her search produced some of the resources we have used in these pages. Another result was the completion of Richards' transformation, in the 1980s, into the truly public woman who could become Governor in the 1990s. It is to the development and education of that public woman that we now turn.

Well, it was such a classic confrontation. You know, it was just so stereotypical, classic, white hat, black hat, and it was not only that— I mean I knew, at the outset, that this race would have more attention than any other race in the country. And I knew that it would have that aspect no matter who my opposition was . . . and it made it even more colorful because Clayton Williams was just, you know, Clayton Williams. And thank God, thank God, they convinced him—Dan Quayle did, Dan Quayle came down here and told him that it was very important for him to remember that he got where he got by being who he was, and not to let these people change him. [We all laugh.] I mean, you know, God in her mercy was working for us.

—GOVERNOR ANN RICHARDS, interview with the authors, 16 October 1991

CHAPTER 2

The Education of a Public Woman

Ann Richards has always been a very funny woman. She has kept friends and political colleagues in stitches for most of her adult life. But Governor Richards has not always been a woman for whom "God in *her* mercy" would roll off the tongue. Her gender consciousness, her feminism, and her sense of herself as an independent individual are all things that have developed over time. With each stage in that development, she has tested and filled a new political role. The evolution of Richards, the leader, clearly follows the evolution of Ann, the woman. But she is also a product both of the Texas political culture into which she was born and bred and of her own interpretation and use of her encounters with that culture.

She was born in the Depression, into the era of the New Deal and the flower of Texas progressivism. She came of political age in the dark 1950s: darkened for women by the loss of opportunities that had seemed to open for them in the 1930s and during World War II, and darkened for Texas politics by the brooding shadows cast by race and class divisions. Richards' beginnings—her childhood socialization to politics that her mother oversaw, her adolescent exposure to a world far larger and more thrilling than that into which she had been born, her young adulthood as the adoring wife of a rising liberal lawyer in the 1950s and 1960s, and her midlife arrival at full personal, political, and feminist maturity—all were shaped by the tapestry of Texas politics, just as she, in turn, has contributed her own weaving to its pattern. And so, before we turn to Ann Richards' life, we will first sketch in the tapestry's design.

Claytie and the Lady

"DOING POLITICS": TRANSFORMATIONS IN THE PARTY SYSTEM, 1940S TO 1980S

Despite strong strains of progressivism, feminism, and populism in the first decades of the twentieth century, Texas politics has rarely featured decisive liberal/conservative ideological struggles, as those terms are usually understood, until quite recently. On questions of race, class, and social welfare, most Texas political elites can only be called conservative. Fehrenbach's (1968) influential history, *Lone Star*, popularized the term "folk conservatism" as a description of the state's political culture, although that fails to do justice to its diversity—not everybody in Texas is, or has been, a cowboy.[1] Strong populist, progressive, and even socialist efforts were mounted continuously from the 1880s to the 1930s, and, as we have seen, these efforts sometimes bore the fruit of more generous social policy. But for almost all of the twentieth century, one-party Democratic politics effectively monopolized political power. That power was acquired and maintained by elites who used it largely for personal aggrandizement, and largely for the maintenance of the status quo. (Nor was the rise of the Republican party and genuine two-party competition in the 1980s to change the picture much.)

As it did for the rest of the nation, Franklin Roosevelt's ascendancy in the 1930s created opportunities for the rise of New Deal liberalism in Texas politics, building on some of the Progressive achievements of the 1920s. By 1944, the struggle for control of the Democratic party had become a pitched battle between conservative elites and liberal Roosevelt loyalists. Liberals began building a network of statewide grass roots organizations. The liberal hope had always been to defeat the Southern "unit rule" (the absolute control by party leaders of delegate blocks at nominating conventions), to end elite domination, and to open nomination processes to the masses—and particularly to people of color—and liberals thought they were about to achieve some of those goals when the United States Supreme Court declared Texas' all-white (Democratic) primary unconstitutional. The defeat of the liberal New Deal gubernatorial candidate Homer Rainey in 1946, however, was to mean that, except for the legendary Ralph Yarborough's tenure in the Senate from 1957 to 1971, liberals would be shut out of party power for almost thirty years. (Davidson 1990: 25, 27, 30), and they were to be shut out of the Governor's Mansion until Ann Richards' victory in 1990.[2]

Both Governor Allan Shivers (who, along with his supporters, called "Shiverites," was farther to the right than present-day Republicans) and Governor John Connally dominated Democratic politics and would eventually become Republicans. They are, as Davidson describes them, "the embodiment of Texas conservatism. Both intelligent and charismatic, they were born poor and got rich quickly, gaining acceptance as peers among the upper class . . ." (1990: 29). They really were thoroughgoing conservatives, as was the most noted Republican for much of the period, John Tower. Unlike Tower, though, Shivers and Connally retained the color, charisma, and personal following that had characterized prewar Texas Governors but could be found in no other major Texas political player, except Lyndon Johnson, until Ann Richards became Governor.[3]

Shivers and the "Shiverites," who had shifted the New Deal–liberal coalition out of power in the 1940s, were shifted themselves in the 1950s—but not by liberals. Instead, Speaker Sam Rayburn and Senator Lyndon Johnson assumed control of the party. Johnson's later civil-rights achievements as President notwithstanding, his relations with the Progressive wing of his state party were bitter in the extreme during this period. But voting rights and civil rights, the milieu of President Johnson's Great Society and the optimism it fostered, national Democratic party reforms beginning in 1968, and the long valor of the "liberal visionaries who fought the trench warfare of Texas convention politics" (Davidson 1990: 178) were to result in the liberals' once more exercising meaningful power within the party. Their grassroots organizations "enabled them to . . . use their most potent resource—'ordinary people' getting together in precinct conventions across the state—to neutralize the effects of the conservatives' money" (ibid).

Although liberals in the Democratic party had long sought the flight of its conservatives to the GOP, to their consternation voters, too, were turning toward the Republicans. That meant that, while Ann Richards could become one of the few authentic liberals to win statewide office in Texas when she was elected Treasurer in 1982, and could win reelection almost breezily in 1986, she had risen to the top ranks of a party that could no longer guarantee success in a gubernatorial general election. Richards' occupancy of the Governor's Mansion as a Democrat, a *liberal*, and worse still a *woman*, would seem wholly improbable. We have seen the political culture arrive at a place where her election could not only seem probable (if unlikely), but could actually happen. But how did Ann Richards arrive at a place from which she could launch the campaign?

THE LIFECOURSE OF A LEADER

Ann Richards spent her childhood and adolescence in the 1930s and 1940s, when progressivism yet had some presence in Texas politics. She was raised in modest circumstances, where prudence and practicality were everything, yet also within sound of her father's tall tales, and with her mother's encouragement to be active, to have public roles, to present her best face to the world. "You know, my mother said that 'No self-respecting woman could possibly have straight hair now that there are Toni home permanents,'" the Governor says, but her mother also saw that she trained in public speaking, and encouraged her civic development (Richards 1989).

Richards' adolescent civic training attained its zenith when she attended Girls' State and Girls' Nation in the late 1940s. At that time, too, she met the young man she would marry, David Richards, and his mother, Eleanor. Eleanor, who had attended Grinnell College and Radcliffe, and who had founded the Waco, Texas, chapter of the League of Women Voters, opened new worlds to eager, impressionable Ann Willis (Richards 1989). Jane Hickie, Richards' friend and colleague since the 1970s, and currently the Executive Director of the Texas Office of Federal Relations, says, "You can just imagine what it was like for her, the first time she met Eleanor Richards, a woman who had been the state President of the

League of Women Voters, and there were *New Yorker* maga-
zines in the [Richards] house . . . the worlds that were opened,
of ideas, and yet . . . the thing that her family has given her is
that Ann is, she is reality. She never strays very far from what
is practical, from what is, from how people really are, how
they really feel" (interview, 21 November 1991).

David and Ann graduated from college in 1954, married,
and moved to Austin, where David attended law school. They
quickly became a part of the Austin Progressive set, interested in civil rights and labor issues. Hickie says that the
three "convergent streams" of intelligence, practicality, and
(grounded, realistic) idealism characteristic of Richards were
evident then, but Richards did not yet believe in her own
independent capacities. Hickie says, "David Richards has
many wonderful qualities. One of them is his immense curiosity about things. I think that when you asked earlier about
her self-esteem and self-confidence, I think one of the things
that she always thought was that David was a lot, lot, lot
smarter than she was." And Ann, with what seems like
boundless energy, nonetheless saw herself first and foremost
as his wife and as a mother. But, Hickie says, "she had always run huge enterprises. I mean, you'd say, well, let's have
a birthday party. Well, it wouldn't be a birthday party, it would
be an extravaganza. I remember one year [after the Richardses
had returned to Austin, in the 1970s] they rented the Arma-
dillo World Headquarters [a now-defunct large and popular
club], and I mean, there must have been four hundred people,
five hundred people there."

This fabled birthday party followed twenty years of extraordinarily organized energy devoted principally to David
Richards and the couple's four children; while politics was at
the center of every adult conversation at home and (from the
impressions one draws from the Governor's autobiography)
every social engagement abroad, Ann Richards yet saw herself as subsidiary to David. After David completed law school,
the Richardses moved to Dallas, where he began practicing
labor law, and she ran a house that was equal parts nursery,
progressive salon, and home away from home for a variety of
political activists whenever any of them descended on conservative Dallas (Richards 1989).

Liberal activists flocked to progressive events in Dallas because that period—the late 1950s and early 1960s—was a time of violent struggles over desegregation in Texas, as it was in the nation, and Ann Richards was moved to pit her energies against racism. Ann worked in (now U.S. Representative) Henry Gonzalez' 1958 gubernatorial campaign, there deepening her passionate advocacy of social justice (Richards 1989: 93–97). She was to become more and more politically involved after that campaign, but always as the willing and energetic yet powerless volunteer: "I don't want to paint my role in these political doings as one of any significance. Most of what I did was make phone calls and stuff envelopes . . . I was a peripheral player," the Governor says (Richards 1989: 117). The election of John F. Kennedy to the presidency, with Lyndon Johnson as his Vice-President, was an exhilarating event for the Richardses, and David took a position as a staff attorney at the Civil Rights Commission. After a year in Washington, the Richardses returned to Dallas and more feverish political involvement.

In the late 1960s, Ann Richards met United Farm Workers organizer Ernie Cortez. His political approach (see Rogers 1990), developed in his tutelage with Saul Alinsky, was profoundly to affect her. She began by working with him to help stop the sale of nonunion melons in Dallas-area grocery stores—without too much success, as she laments in her autobiography. His philosophy, shared by Richards and her closest associates, such as former Chief of Staff Mary Beth Rogers, emphasizes the importance of compromise, of not leaving the table with nothing, of putting normative concerns aside in favor of pragmatic assessments of what *can* be done, and of "never doing for people what they can do for themselves" (Cartwright 1991; Rogers 1990). Perhaps her mature approach to politics, as a public woman herself, took root in these experiences, after the seed of practicality was sown in her childhood. Such an approach has certainly marked her leadership orientations as State Treasurer and as Governor. What she might not have realized at this time was that her fundamental orientations toward political practice would diverge more and more from those of her husband David.

THE EDUCATION OF A PUBLIC WOMAN

The late 1960s were also formative for Richards in other ways. In 1968 liberals began what, in a few short years, would lead to control of the Democratic party, a "pushing out" of conservatives, who fell into the arms of the Republicans. In 1969 the Richardses left Dallas, never congenial to them, and returned to their beloved Austin, where the heart of renascent feminism in Texas was also emerging. While she did not at first feel any comfortable connections to new feminists, such as Hickie, or even to "old" ones such as Liz Carpenter, she could not have found a more fruitful environment for her own eventual feminist resocialization. With the move, Ann had, in fact, vowed that she would have no more to do with politics, since "it was painfully clear [that] women weren't going to be allowed to use their brains and I certainly wanted to use mine" (Richards 1989: 136). Only two years after her return to Austin, though, she was approached by the young Sarah Weddington and asked to manage her campaign for the Texas legislature. Hickie says:

> *Running Sarah's campaign [which Weddington won], working over there in the legislature [as Weddington's administrative assistant], then she ran Wilhelmina [Delco]'s campaign [which Delco won, becoming the first black person to represent Austin in the state legislature], and then she got involved in the [Henry] Gonzales race [for Congress], and helped them. You know, she had become like the political wizard, the person who could help figure out how to run campaigns, how to get that money in the door, from West Austin, for minority candidates. She became a big deal. Times are much different, but she and David were like a, they were joined at the hip. And so, this is really hard to believe, I hope this is true, I'm not sure, but I think it is, among the men, Ann would do something, so that meant David is the one they'd talk to. That must mean that David is really smart politically.*

> *And I'm not sure that Ann didn't do some things*
> *that contributed to that picture. (Interview, 21*
> *November 1991)*

Taking over the management of Weddington's campaign, Richards quickly demonstrated the "androgynous" characteristics that have strongly marked women who are successful in the electoral arena. On the one hand, she had imaginative flair and could make a lot of a little—often thought to be "women's skills." At one candidate rally, for example, she worried about what to give potential voters, short on funds as the campaign was, since she knew that other campaigns would distribute stickers, buttons, brochures, pens and pencils, and other paraphernalia. She hit upon the idea of offering voters plain paper bags to put their other paraphernalia in, and these bags, with Weddington's name and autograph on them, in turn became the hit of the rally (Tolchin and Tolchin 1974 [this work also marks Richards' first appearance in a national mainstream book on women and politics]; Richards 1989).

On the other hand, she was not at all "traditionally feminine" in her deep respect for hard, shrewd political research. She knew, much earlier than did most women venturing into the electoral arena, that there is no substitute for the dull but essential work of precinct analysis, voter targeting, careful strategy, and incessant planning. The liberal *Texas Observer* dubbed her the Weddington campaign's "political brain trust," and she was "so happy to be referred to as a political brain trust, not just a housewife," Weddington said (Tolchin and Tolchin 1974: 190).

Then came one of what Hickie calls the "epiphanies" in Richards' evolution: she ran for office herself, as Travis County Commissioner—but only after *David* had been asked, and had turned the offer down. Hickie thinks that, in those times, Ann's successes were seen as David's:

> *That's why, when she says that they came to David*
> *and asked David to run for Commissioner, I mean*
> *David's smart, and he has that presence, he has a*
> *real commanding presence, and he had that fabu-*

lous wife who'd know how to raise money and how to make it work, and how to put the numbers together . . . and so David would go out there and talk, he's really an intelligent, competent, excellent lawyer, and Ann would run the campaign. It's perfect. I mean, I'll bet you dollars to doughnuts, that's what they had in their minds. When David said somebody here has to make a living, or "I don't want to do that," they said, "Well, Ann, why don't you do it?" Major turning point. They went to the beach, you know, that's a real home for her, to go to the beach at South Padre [Island, on the Gulf coast], and talk about it. And they had numbers. She had told people how to do the targeting, she wanted to look at the numbers and see if she could win. Now see how realistic that is! She didn't go down there with David to talk about, I don't know really what they talked about, but not exclusively, "Is this going to screw up getting your shirts laundered?" or, I mean, she has brought a set of numbers precinct by precinct to analyze whether she can win [Hickie laughs]. Now that is what makes her different. If you have had any dealings with women candidates who are running for local office, most of them, you have to tell them that there is such a thing as precinct analysis. They are clueless that you don't get elected to office just because you're for the Equal Rights Amendment . . . What [voters] care about is whether or not they have potholes . . . That's a revolutionary notion that Ann Richards understands, but that many women candidates to this day don't understand. So that was key. She goes down there, she decides to run. (Interview, 21 November 1991)

In her own campaign, even more than in her work for Weddington, Delco, and Gonzales, she exhibited a combination of traditional "feminine" and "masculine" traits that added up to a vital sense of what works in politics. Some have assumed, for example, that women candidates prefer to run *for* themselves, rather than *against* opponents—that women, in short, "don't like to be negative" (see a discussion of such assumptions in Welch and Studlar 1990; see also Note 4 of this chapter). But Richards recognized early that she would have to identify and exploit her opponent's weak points if she were to unseat a well-known incumbent. Throughout her political career, she has never shirked "negative" campaigning, even if she does not relish it. She knows the rules of the political game too well. She also "did the numbers," determining, for example, who in her Travis County district had voted for Sissy Farenthold in the gubernatorial primaries of 1972 and 1974, who had voted for women or minority men in city council elections, and who had shown up at the polls in city bond and referendum elections with very low turnouts. From this research she carefully estimated which precinct "boxes" she could win, which she couldn't, and which she could take a shot at (Mandel 1981: 131–132; Richards 1989: 156–161).

But when she "walked the block" in her precisely targeted precincts, she also did "feminine" things, things male candidates might not so readily think to do. If a voter was not at home, she would note some feature of the house or garden, and leave the note with her brochure. In one case this attention to detail produced unanticipated results. She had left a note praising the beauty of the household calico cat and asking the householders to let her know should the cat ever have kittens. Some time later, the startled Richards received a call telling her that her calico kitten was ready to be fetched. Composing herself, she accepted the gift (Richards 1989; Mandel 1981).

Appraising the sentiments of her district and its likely voters, she also devoted care to presenting herself as a pleasant-looking, modestly affluent housewife and mother, as someone *like* them, and committed to being *accessible* to them—a homemaker who would be a careful steward. Even Congressman Jim Mattox, who was to become Texas Attorney General in the 1980s and Richards' bitterest primary foe in the 1990 gubernatorial race, thought his own Democratic primary opponent of the time, Nancy Judy, was "a fool not to make use of her housewife's expertise on bill paying, the high cost of living, and the problems created by inflation" (Mandel 1981: 56).

The early 1970s was a time of spectacular new energy in women's political activities. This was the time when the number of women elected to state and local office was to increase from the almost immeasurably small numbers of the 1950s and 1960s (women's share of legislative seats actually *declined* from 1963 to 1972; Darcy, Welch, and Clark 1987: 48) to the larger (but still tiny) bases—8% of state legislative seats, 4% of local offices—against which we have since measured women's progress. (These 1975 figures are from the Center for the American Woman and Politics 1991.) Ann Richards' emergence as a feminist was yet in the future, but her campaign management and candidacy in the early 1970s unquestionably made her one of the visible trailblazers of the new era of women's electoral success.

It was also during Richards' campaign for County Commissioner that, according to Hickie, she and Ann Richards first became close. Jane Hickie had helped found the Austin chapter of the National Women's Political Caucus. Richards had been an early member—after all, it was another progressive political group. But in 1974, Richards had resigned bitterly from the caucus. Hickie recalls the event, and their subsequent reconnection during Richards' campaign for the Travis County Commission:

> We had a big fight over Jake Pickle running against
> [Progressive] Larry Bales [for Congress], and Ann
> Richards thought we were terrible not to be for
> Larry Bales. But we were for Jake Pickle. That year
> the only people who had endorsed Jake Pickle were
> the Women's Political Caucus and the plumbers and
> pipefitters [union]. So she was still very much . . . it
> was like Ann and David and those people were the
> liberals and the labor people and like that. They
> were West Austin, and very faculty, UT, you know,
> chi chi, lawyers, very—like that. The women stuff:
> Sarah [Weddington] did that. That was Sarah's
> thing. And the women's organizations were . . .
> they were young women, just out of college, or they

> *were old firebrands like Liz Carpenter. And there*
> *was very little of a middle deal except it was sort of*
> *like League of Women Voters people who would*
> *drop by and really weren't sure what this was*
> *about. And so Ann thought all of this stuff was just*
> *like, "I don't know what you're doing over here" . . .*
> *she felt like all this "women stuff" somehow, it*
> *wasn't like labor, or faculty, or the groups with*
> *whom she felt comfortable, because, why would*
> *they endorse Jake Pickle, for God's sake, who was*
> *the conservative in the race? And somehow these*
> *crazy women just had an agenda that she wasn't*
> *sure she understood or appreciated.*

As Mary Beth Rogers remembers that time, Richards was distressed not over the caucus' endorsement of Jake Pickle, but over its failure to endorse Democrat Cathy Bonner's candidacy for the state legislature. Perhaps the Governor disliked both actions. Nonetheless, once Richards had decided to make the 1976 race for County Commissioner, Hickie got a telephone call:

> *She calls me up. She wanted to know where the hell*
> *the women are. And I quote. She said, "Here I am*
> *running for County Commissioner, and where the*
> *hell are the women?" And I said, "We didn't know*
> *you wanted any." Just real horsey. I said, "If you*
> *invited any of the women's groups to have anything*
> *to do with your high political councils, and sit down*
> *there at the table where all of those decisions were*
> *made, maybe more of them would have been there.*
> *But, now that you want us to come help, I assure*
> *you that you will be covered up with women want-*
> *ing to volunteer." That was the first conversation*
> *that I remember having with Ann directly . . .*
> *Everything else had been "Hi, how are you?" I had*
> *some early conversations with her in '70 about how*
> *to run a campaign, but she was sort of lecturing,*
> *and it wasn't anything direct . . . Now it's never*

stopped . . . you'd think I'd've quit after that [she chuckles] . . . (Interview, 21 November 1991)

Richards won that first race for the Travis County Commission, of course, and began to be known in the state and in national politics far more than one would expect of a mere County Commissioner. Mandel (1981: 135) argued that on a "global scale, Richards' 'empire' is a modest one, encompassing seventy thousand voters and three hundred square miles of Austin and the surrounding limestone and live-oak hill country. But she scored a rare success: not many first-time candidates for competitive positions offering high status and a good salary manage to win either a primary or a general election in which they unseat a well-known incumbent." That success is the more striking when one considers that of all the significant factors thought to hamper women's election to public office—the occupational "eligibility pool," political background and experience, method of election, the strength of incumbent advantage, cultural hostility toward women in politics, and the value (measured by salary and/or prestige) of the office—only one factor, that of her past political background, worked to Richards' advantage.[4] She overcame all the other obstacles with skill, sheer hard work, toughness, and remarkable political instincts (of both "masculine" and "feminine" varieties). It is no wonder, then, that "only" a Texas County Commissioner would begin to attract so much national attention.

Her conversion to genuine feminist orientations was by now very close on the horizon as well. According to Hickie, her gender consciousness was raised another level when she first attended a national meeting of women in elected office (one of the first such conferences sponsored by the Center for the American Woman and Politics at Rutgers University):

I went to work for her as her aide, and I dropped out of all my women's stuff, women's organizations, all of it . . . I think it was really important to her that I do. I think she was real worried that I was involved in all those women's organizations, in fact I'm sure of it . . . She didn't really understand who [the feminist organizations] were or what they did, but she felt like all this "women stuff," somehow it wasn't like labor, or faculty, the groups with whom she felt comfortable . . . and somehow these crazy women just had an agenda that she wasn't sure she understood or appreciated . . . So she started getting asked to go places and do things, and one of the first things that happened, because she had run such an outstanding campaign, and she was one of the few women, local elected officials, who understood how she got there, she was asked to speak to women's groups: "How did you do it?" An absolute epiphany occurred for her, I think, when she was invited to [this meeting]. And it was . . . right in this same time period, that it was the first time she had ever rented a car, the first time that she ever checked into a hotel [by herself], the first time that she'd ever got on an airplane all by herself, all alone, and she goes to a meeting of other women, elected officials, and there they all are. And they are real smart women, who know other things, and it wasn't some sort of rabble-rousing youngsters and old battleaxes, it was her peers. Here's a city council member from Kansas City, and here's a county commissioner from some other county, around the United States, and these were finally, I think she walked into that room and felt some real common kinship. All of a sudden, some of the women's issues began to make some more sense to her. She began to have greater interest. It began to be a more personal question, and a query . . .

For the first time, perhaps, Richards—who had compassionately identified with African- and Mexican-American people twenty years earlier—could comfortably identify as a woman, with women, even as a feminist.

But, as Hickie and Richards both tell it, these were also the years when her life was nearing a crisis. She was trying to be, and appeared to be, Superwoman. Hickie continues:

*So then she was asked to speak, and she had a real
good speech on "how I got elected," and campaign
techniques, and it was so great. She'd go out and
talk to these groups about how to keep a man. How
to keep your husband interested. Classic. Oh, she
will kill me. Stuff like "read the sports pages"
[Hickie is dissolving in merry laughter as she relates
the story] and you'd look around the room, at state
employees, or teachers, or whoever, and you knew
they had come, just desperate, they were getting
paid nothing, they were being treated like dogs, it
was horrible, and their hope for the future gets up
and tells them a lot of just what they are hoping to
hear, and then tells them that what they need to do
is . . . I mean this was the Superwoman period. You
remember? And she would give a speech where she
ran through this very funny thing about Superwoman, and Superwoman gets up and fixes the
perfect breakfast for her 2.7 children, and is multior-
gasmic all night, and goes to her fulfilling job, and
has intelligent conversation with her husband . . .
Well, I know for a fact, I don't know about the
personal stuff, of course, but I know for a fact that
she was still going home at night and doing two
dinners. The kids would have dinner, and she would
be there with the children while they ate, and then
she and David would have dinner later so they
could have a conversation with each other. And
she's up at five in the morning and out running a
road crew [one of her duties as a County Commis-
sioner] and giving a hundred speeches, and she is
out living that life. The speech would contain the
joke within it, but it still contained the life to which
she aspired. (Interview, 21 November 1991)*

The more quixotic political ideals of David and their
friends increasingly jarred with her growing understanding
and appreciation of real-world politics—indeed, despite the
fact that her idealistic commitment to social justice had never
dimmed, she had always been an extremely practical, goal-

directed person, and this quite significant facet of her personality found exuberant expression in her role as an office holder. Jane Hickie says that the "three streams" of intelligence, practicality, and an idealism now focused on feminist identification with women "really do turn up again and again and again" in Richards' life. By the late 1970s, "David and their friends, the faculty crowd, she thought of as intelligent. The courthouse [where the Travis County Commission sits] is the practical real world, and the women's movement, women's politics, women elected officials were the ones who impressed her, it was never anyone other than the ones who were elected to office. Except people who could write, people who could speak, people who could put things in a particular way. That would be the idealism [for her]."

As extraordinary as Richards' life seemed in the late 1970s and into the early 1980s, though, the appearance masked a rapidly fracturing reality: alcoholism and the slow dissolution of a marriage described as an "institution," a marriage that had very much defined who she saw as her most important self. The Governor says in her autobiography, "Things were not improving in our marriage. David and I never fought, which was probably a failing rather than a blessing. We rarely had arguments, but the marriage was slipping beyond my grasp, and as it did I drank more and more. I don't want to suggest that that was the cause of my drinking. I only know that the pain of living was less with alcohol . . . I thought I would die if I were not married to David Richards . . . Jane Hickie watched my deterioration and was determined to do something about it" (1989: 202, 204). As Hickie says, " . . . it was a very, very, very terrible time for her. She was very, very sick . . . it was not as though Ann was ever not at work. She was not only at work; she was doing the work of fifty! But it wasn't good. Her life was not good." Hickie, other friends, two of the Richards children, and David intervened, confronting her with her alcoholism, and telling her that they had already made arrangements for her treatment in St. Mary's Hospital in Minneapolis (Richards 1989: 206–210).

During her recovery, and the series of separations that led to her 1984 divorce from David after thirty years of marriage, Hickie says, "There began to be some real resonance

[with] the pain that women felt," and Richards had her next "epiphany." Upon her return from treatment in Minnesota, she wanted to make her first priority saving the marriage. But between the time of treatment and the ultimate failure of her marriage, she found herself irresistibly drawn, by her energy, her seeming inability *not* to become engaged by things, and her growing identification with women into the astonishing Texas Women in History project (now on permanent display at the Blagg-Huey Library of Texas Woman's University in Denton). She had thought she was beginning the project for her daughters—she was struck when, having taken her youngest daughter, Ellen, to an exhibit of Texana, Ellen "tugged at [her] sleeve and said 'Where were all the women?'" (Richards 1989: 190). She and Hickie both told us that, although she may have begun it for them, it had become something for her. Hickie explains the "moment" of integration that the project became for Richards:

> *It was a terrible time for her. In the middle of all of that came to fruition a Women in History project. Between the time of going to treatment and going through her divorce, right in [this] time there was the . . . project. I will never forget the night she got up and said what I thought was absolutely, exactly, really true: that she had begun this project to benefit her children and along the way, somehow, it had become something that was for herself. And that was when it became a combination of the, all of those strains came together, and she was sober, and getting well. And here was a historical context: I mean, you weren't just crazy. Women had been doing this forever. And you could be real proud about it. And it just came in a moment of time for her. It really was reaffirming, that she could be. Without this relationship [with David] that had been it.*

When Richards was asked to run for State Treasurer in 1982, after the incumbent Democratic office holder, Warren G. Harding, appeared headed for an indictment, Hickie says:

> *[S]he got up, and went to work at it, and I think*
> *discovered along the way that running for office,*
> *tackling things that she never thought she could,*
> *taking on hard jobs and conquering them, was going*
> *to be a focus for her . . . And she did it. She did it as*
> *an independent woman . . . Ann began to get her*
> *life back together in a way that was new. Really*
> *affirmative . . . a fusion took place . . . she never*
> *was uneasy again about the world of women's*
> *politics . . . (Interview, 21 November 1991)*

Richards campaigned hard all over the state, won the Democratic nomination, campaigned even harder, and won the election with 61.4% of the vote. She was the first woman to have been elected to statewide office in Texas since Miriam "Ma" Ferguson had won the gubernatorial election of 1932. And by the time she won, she had become the very gender-conscious, woman-identified, unabashedly feminist, but still inimitable Ann Richards who would, ten years later, tell women to "write a check for just one good pair of Ferragamo shoes" to the Dianne Feinstein and Barbara Boxer campaigns, and who would introduce herself to the 1992 Democratic Nominating Convention, for which she served as chairperson, with the words, "My name is Ann Richards. I'm pro-choice, and I vote."

Between the early 1970s, just before the time of Richards' election to the Travis County Commission, and her election as Governor of Texas, the number of women in state legislatures had more than quadrupled, from 344 (or 4.5% of all legislators) in 1971 to 1,365 (or over 18% of all legislators) in 1991; the total leaped again in the 1992 elections. The number of women in the U.S. House had risen from 16 to 29 by 1991 (and had grown by 20 in 1992). It was not until 1992, after Richards' success in 1990, that the number of women in the Senate rose from 2 to 6 (the number at the time of writing is 7, with Texas Republican Kay Bailey Hutchison's success in the June 1993 special election, replacing Senate Democrat Lloyd Bentsen. This, paradoxically, is another example of how Richards' victory in 1990 has contributed to the credibility of later women's candidacies for high office, regardless of the fact that, in this case, Hutchison's gain was Richards' loss, since the Governor could not retain Bentsen's Democratic seat.) The national average number of women holding statewide elective office had also approximately doubled during the same two-decade period, increasing to 20% of all such offices in 1992, from about 10% in the mid-1970s (figures from the Center for the American Woman and Politics). Richards had, of course, contributed to that increase, as a two-term Treasurer.

While she could follow in the path of the women Governors who had served before her—from Ella Grasso in the 1970s to Madeleine Kunin (Democrat of Vermont) and Kay Orr (Republican of Nebraska) in the late 1980s—Richards has been more the pathbreaker in her own right than the beneficiary of a trend. She had been one of the most skilled of the women who burst onto state and local electoral scenes in the mid-1970s, and was the first to end the long dearth of women in statewide office in Texas since Ma Ferguson. As Richards was achieving and holding statewide office, moreover, Texas was badly lagging behind most of the nation in terms of women's share of local and state legislative offices. Despite her visibility, and the visibility of some others, such as Houston Mayor Kathy Whitmire, the proportion of women in the Texas legislature only progressed from 4% of all seats in 1975 to a still paltry 8.8% in 1985 (Darcy, Welch, and Clark 1987: 47), and after Barbara Jordan left the U.S. House of Representatives, Texas did not have another female member in its congressional delegation until 1992. Electoral politics has remained a difficult business for women—and increasingly so the higher the office. In Texas, what is "difficult" for women elsewhere sometimes seems impossible. This is what makes Ann Richards' electoral career so significant. Her passage through the Texas political crucible is a case study not just for Texans, but for all students of women's progress through electoral arenas. Writing two decades ago, Jeane Kirkpatrick (1974: 218–239) could even then point out that, contrary to gendered stereotypes, "public women" were both "feminine" and *very* similar to political men in their ego strength, their efficacy,

Claytie and the Lady

their realism, their participatory orientations, and their competence. We would certainly see Ann Richards here. Where public women differed, though, Kirkpatrick said, was in their role constraints: in terms of help, they expected little, asked for little, and got little, particularly from spouses. There, too, we can see the Ann Richards of twenty years ago. Today, she expects, asks, and gets a great deal of everyone around her. Quick-tempered, fast-moving, and tough, yet with undeniably "feminine" warmth and the quality of being engaged by people, she may offer one of the strongest contemporary examples of the androgynous combination of traits most necessary to a "public woman's" success.

READY TO RUN

Ann Richards' life is in many ways a classic American example of a political elite's eventual socialization through the life course, from early civic training to, ultimately, national-level political office. Deeply influenced by the New Deal political environment in her childhood, her Democratic partisanship developed early and persisted with tenacity, as it did for many in her generation (see, for example, Jennings and Markus 1984). This helped form her core orientations to politics. This alone, however, might only describe someone who votes regularly but otherwise is uninterested and uninvolved in politics. Our understanding of Ann Richards' evolution into a public woman requires much more thought.

Her practical, down-to-earth mother and her yarn-spinning father helped forge the personality that she would present to the world, but her mother in particular made sure that civic roles and responsibilities would be important outlets for the young Ann's energies. Through childhood and adolescence, she was a joiner, a participator: we know that this general participatory orientation is very strongly associated with political engagement (see Jennings and Niemi 1981; Sigel and Hoskin 1981; Beck and Jennings 1982; Beck and Jennings 1988).

She had two experiences in adolescence, however, that

she and her friends saw as exceptionally formative—an assertion with which any scholar of political socialization would agree. These experiences were her attendance at Girls' State and Girls' Nation and her informal political tutelage at the knee of Eleanor Richards. For someone who already had a strong, innate impulse toward engagement and an as-yet-inchoate passion for social justice, these opportunities were gifts indeed. Intelligent, activist young people rapidly respond to whatever cues and lessons their environments offer them; this has been, if anything, the more true for young women with a political bent, particularly in times when they must seek especially hard for models of "political woman" (Tolleson Rinehart 1985).

Had she been a young *man*, attending *Boys'* State and *Boys'* Nation—as President Bill Clinton did—it would have been simple to foretell for her a career in politics or public affairs. She was not a young man, of course, and she did what most women of her generation did: she married, raised children, and devoted herself to the making of a home—although, because she is Ann Richards, simple "homemaking" was transformed into the production of one extravaganza after another, and the creation of the modern-day version of a political salon. For Ann and David, as is true of very few American families in the twentieth century (though it was true much more often in the nineteenth century, at least for men), politics remained a significant avocation, a huge source of entertainment and social connection, and an important part of their vision of the good life. Ann Richards was never politically inactive in the late 1950s and 1960s, and in the 1970s her involvement only grew: after the Richards family returned to Austin, she began to integrate her interests and passions with sharp organizational skills. In this way, the socialization toward political engagement begun in her childhood continued the upward spiraling we would expect to see: it is rare to find someone who, politicized early in life, withdraws from political involvement later in the life cycle.

But a major task of *resocialization* also lay before her in the 1970s: that of her own reconceptualization of her roles, toward gender consciousness and feminism. Before she con-

structed these new cognitive frameworks from which to understand her own political impulses and the kinds of political roles she *really* wanted to play, her political activism had
been quite traditionally gendered. Consider her party and
campaign work until the early 1970s: here she fit a model
that gender politics scholars have long understood, a model
of women's "housekeeping" and selfless service in the public realm, built on what women had always contributed to
the private domain. As Carroll (1989: 313–314) argues, "the
gender-specific nature of women's involvement in conventional politics may reflect the effects of gender-based socialization on women's political aspirations and motivations for
involvement . . . While men saw their involvement [in political parties] as a 'vehicle for personal enhancement and career
advancement,' women viewed their involvement as a 'labor
of love' through which they could serve others . . ." (see also
Costantini and Craik 1977; Fowlkes, Perkins, and Tolleson
Rinehart 1979; Jennings and Farah 1981). This "labor of love"
was something she had been trained and was inclined to provide—and was in any case virtually all that men in politics
would have been willing to accept from women at the time—
but in the course of the 1970s, she and thousands of other
women could no longer suppress the frustrated feeling that
political "housekeeping" just was not enough. At the same
time, the Texas political culture, like that of the nation as a
whole, was slowly opening itself to acceptance of precisely
the larger, truly empowered roles that women wanted to play.

Richards' election to the Travis County Commission was
a watershed event, or, as Jane Hickie terms it, an "epiphany"
in her life. Her role, now, was to be a player, and not just a
woman (no matter how smart and savvy) serving the players.
But, as we know, she began by *adding* this role to her earlier
ones: now she was the perfect wife and mother *and* office
holder. She joked about "Superwoman," but Superwoman she
was nonetheless trying to be. Only the searing experiences
of confronting her alcoholism and surviving the end of her
marriage, all while immersing herself in the Texas Women
in History project, forged the final understanding of herself
as a truly independent woman who yet could eagerly iden-

tify with women. A less strong woman might not have been able to extract such understanding from such pain. She did. Her election as State Treasurer in 1982 provided a triumphant opportunity to exercise this new knowledge of herself and her place as a public woman. By the end of the 1980s, she was uniquely prepared to make the leap into a gubernatorial campaign.

We Democrats believe that America is still the country of fair play, that we can come out of a small town or a poor neighborhood and have the same chance as anyone else, and it doesn't matter whether we're black or Hispanic, disabled or female.

—ANN RICHARDS, keynote address to the 1988 Democratic Nominating Convention

[Campaign staff] claim that they didn't tell [Richards] she couldn't be funny [during the campaign, when it seemed that all the laughter disappeared for a time]. Ann told me that nobody would let her, that it was death to be funny. And she's very . . . you know, part of it is proving you're tough enough, that goes back to the glass ceiling thing, is a woman tough enough for a big job like Governor? Think of the amount of cultural expectation attached to a title like "Governor." And what you invariably get is the tall, distinguished, white-haired man . . .

—MOLLY IVINS, interview with the authors, 14 May 1991

CHAPTER 3

Campaign Strategies

Ann Richards' victory in the 1990 Texas gubernatorial election imbued her keynote address comment two years earlier with symbolic meaning: a woman of modest small-town origins had journeyed all the way to the Governor's Mansion, emerging triumphantly from one of the most searing political crucibles in the country. But the substance of the campaign belied the limpid simplicity of that message of equality, and, as Molly Ivins noted, day-to-day circumstances were often so grim that even Richards' humor, perhaps the thing for which she is most widely known, had disappeared from view. The reality had been that her sex, and her past, *had* mattered. Indeed, had her Republican opponent Clayton Williams not made so many errors—mistakes that, in the end, forced him into the uncharacteristic position of humbly apologizing to voters and pleading for their support—few think that Ann Richards, a liberal and a woman, could have become Governor. Her keynote address at the 1988 Democratic Nominating Convention is memorable to most people for the "silver foot in his mouth" remark about George Bush ("Claytie" was later to use a television commercial repeating that particular sound bite and admonishing her for criticizing the President). Although many people found the remark to be humorous, other Texans (of both sexes) were strongly critical of her for making it, not least because it could be interpreted as unseemly behavior for a "lady." (Some think that humor has also rebounded unfavorably on other prominent political women, such as U.S. Representative Patricia Schroeder or 1984 Democratic vice-presidential candidate

Claytie and the Lady

Geraldine Ferraro.) Thus, while Richards, as a woman, was a thrilling inspiration to many, the high profiles of both the sex of the candidates and gendered interpretations of the candidates' sex were controversial, and never simple or straightforward in their meaning.

Williams tried to evoke Texas' wide-open cowboy past and almost succeeded, although centrally placed Republicans later felt that packaging Williams this way was a serious mistake (see Massett interview, 13 May 1991; Rister interview, 3 August 1993). Richards, notwithstanding her own deep roots in traditional Texas culture, nonetheless called for a "New Texas" of business savvy and populist inclusiveness, of tough management and compassion. But much of Texas is not "new": traditional social conservatism, especially with regard to conventional gender roles, remains robust in most of the state. Richards had come to political maturity in the liberal progressive circles of Dallas and Austin, and was lauded almost universally as one of the most effective State Treasurers in Texas history. In order to become Governor, though, she faced the puzzle of appearing tough enough, and yet not too removed from "appropriate" femininity, progressive and forward-looking, and yet not too "liberal" (the favorite pejorative of Texas politics in the last decade).

Richards' longtime friend, political associate, and first Chief of Staff Mary Beth Rogers believes that her two terms as State Treasurer had prepared the way for a considerable amount of attitude transformation:

> Let me start with voter perceptions. Voters expect both more and less of a female. They expect a greater degree of competency, a greater degree of honesty, so in some sense they expect more on a personal level from a woman than a man, I think. On the other hand, they're surprised when a woman knows as much as a man, [has] an equal amount of expertise. What we found . . . we did extensive polling in the [gubernatorial] campaign—we reversed certain stereotypical perceptions. Voters rarely felt that women had the financial expertise to hold high office, yet they felt Ann Richards had greater financial expertise and greater knowledge of

*governing than Clayton Williams. And so that
reversal of a stereotypical role ended up helping us,
but that's not the way it usually is—that happened
to be because she was Treasurer; we learned in the
Treasurer's [races] that voters were more inclined to
allow women to handle money in government than
just about any other function, because they trusted
in the honesty of women at a greater level than
[they trusted] men. (Interview, 15 October 1991)*

Richards' campaign staff had deliberately worked to present an image of her as the (political) chief executive of a large enterprise, with all the cool, savvy competence that image implies: all her strategists were conscious of the need to stimulate the kinds of "stereotypical role reversals" that Rogers so pointedly referred to. But presenting an image and having that image broadly accepted can be two quite different things, even though, with her hard, unblinking political instincts, Richards never would have made the race had she not been convinced that there was a chance she could win. Nonetheless, she always had her work cut out for her.

In the end, Clayton Williams made her job easier by finally breaking the "cowboy code" so many times that he became unacceptable to many who would otherwise have been his natural—and loyal—Republican constituency. While many voters stayed home on election day, and while many who did vote professed disgust with the whole campaign, the outcome—49.6% for Richards, 47.1% for Williams, and 3.3% for a Libertarian candidate (figures from the Secretary of State)—showed that while "Claytie" could not outdistance the voter distaste that eventually accumulated against him, Richards did succeed, albeit barely, in overcoming the obstacle of negative perceptions of her that had left her campaign near despair some months before the election.

AN APPROACH TO UNDERSTANDING GENDER IN POLITICAL CAMPAIGNS

Perceptions of gender roles, as most observers and insiders agreed, held a position of unusual importance in this race

(Gillman 1990; Suro 1990; McNeely 1990; Germond and Witcover 1990). We have argued from the outset that gender-role perceptions both helped and harmed each candidate: gender-role traditionalists were discomfited by the idea of a woman Governor, especially one so clearly linked in the public eye to feminism. At the same time, Williams' virtually legendary gaffes—his unfortunate joke that bad weather was like rape, his discussion of being "serviced" by prostitutes in his youth, his refusal to shake Richards' (the "lady's") hand—deeply offended many traditionalists as well as those of a more egalitarian bent. (They will be presented in all their lurid detail in the next chapter.) Many egalitarians were ardent Richards supporters from the very beginning—feminist volunteers were a sturdy backbone to her campaign—and yet she had to reach out to others as well, persuading them that she embodied the difficult combination of strength and toughness, compassion and accessibility that voters presently expect from women candidates, especially those running for political chief executive positions (Pierce 1989; Huddy and Terkildsen 1993; Huddy and Terkildsen 1993a).

But most attempts to assess the significance of the sex of the candidate and that of the gender-role orientations of the voter and candidate are too simple to do justice to an extraordinarily complex set of phenomena. It is not merely a question of simple virtual representation—of getting more women into high offices—or even of substantive representation—of securing a place for so-called "women's issues" on the public agenda (and this, you will notice, makes some pretty strong assumptions of its own that all women in office will be "everywoman," and that men could not advocate "women's" issues). Any woman candidate, any woman officeholder, in our gendered world, is a "symbolic woman" (Sapiro 1993), and beyond—or within—questions of democratic theory or public policy making, these symbolic women are seen, judged, responded to through the prisms of gender (we specify the plural "prisms," because the meanings of gender and gender roles are highly variable). As the social psychologists Kay Deaux and Brenda Major put it (1987: 369–370), any useful understanding of the role that gender plays in the relations of human beings to one another must emphasize "the extent to

which gender-linked social behaviors are multiply determined, highly flexible, and context dependent," arising
from culture and distant childhood learning about gender
roles, but even more importantly from proximate circumstances. The Deaux and Major model encompasses a number
of elements:

> *This model proposes a hypothesized sequence of
> events but does not represent a causal model in the
> statistical sense. It contains three key elements: (a)
> a perceiver, who enters the interaction with a set of
> beliefs about gender and with personal interaction
> goals; (b) a target individual, who enters the interac-
> tion with his or her own gender-related self-concep-
> tions and interaction goals; and (c) a situation,
> which can vary in the degree to which it makes
> gender-related issues salient . . . [P]erceivers ap-
> proach situations with a set of beliefs about the
> target—beliefs that are based on categorical as-
> sumptions or that derive from past experience with
> the particular individual . . . These beliefs . . . can be
> activated by a variety of factors . . . Influenced by
> these beliefs as well as by specific interaction goals,
> the perceiver then acts toward the target . . .
> Shifting to the vantage point of the target or the
> self, we suggest that targets enter situations with
> a set of beliefs about themselves, particular aspects
> of which may be activated by factors similar to
> those that affect the perceiver . . . After interpreting
> the actions of the perceiver . . . the target then
> weighs possible alternatives and takes some action
> in accord with his or her interaction goals—action
> that may either confirm or disconfirm the beliefs of
> the perceiver . . . This interaction sequence is far
> from invariant, and its course is affected by two
> general classes of modifying conditions . . . First,
> characteristics of the transmitted expectancy may
> vary. Of specific importance to this model are the
> social desirability of the expected behavior, the
> certainty with which the expectancy is held by the

> *perceiver, and the degree to which it is conveyed by
> situational cues. A second set of modifying condi-
> tions concerns the relative balance between the
> target's concerns with self-presentation and self-
> verification [the interweaving of private and public
> identity]. To complete the cycle . . . the model
> considers the perceiver's interpretation of the
> target's action . . . and the target's interpretations of
> his or her own actions. (1987: 371–372)*

Deaux and Major further note that "characteristics of the immediate situation are a third influence on the activation of gender-related expectancies . . . The salience of the target vis-à-vis other aspects of the situation also increases the probability that gender-related schemata will be activated . . . Consequently, perceivers interacting with the only woman among a group of men or the only man among a group of women may be particularly likely to activate expectancies with respect to the target's sex" (p. 374) especially because "it is virtually impossible for a person to be 'sex blind' . . . As a consequence, the gender belief system may be activated very quickly, before other potentially contradictory information can be introduced" (p. 384).

The Deaux and Major approach says, in short, that when two people meet, each thinks, "That is a woman/man" before almost anything else, while at virtually the same time thinking, "I am a woman/man: how is that person responding to this?" and, "Because I am a woman/man, how am I expected to act in this situation?" These thoughts are almost instantaneous, and often not fully conscious. And the "He's responding to me this way because I am a woman" and "Should a woman be doing this?" adjustments are being made constantly, as the interaction progresses. They also depend not only on each person's preconceived attitudes, and on the verbal interaction between them, but on even more subtle things as well, such as appearance, gesture, and dress. In other words, our behavior is being constantly influenced by the fact that we "know" that others "know" we are male or female and are presenting ourselves accordingly, trying to meet others' expectations about our sex as well as expectations of our own. We may not even do or say what we, on our own, would like to do or say, if it seems more important that we behave as "appropriate" women or men in a given context.

Deaux and Major could hardly have imagined a more intricate case upon which to test their model than the 1990 Texas gubernatorial campaign. Consider only two of numerous facets of the case: first, *politics* is the context, messy, pejorative, *male* politics; and second, there is the question of Clayton Williams' "manhood." Most people, giving thought to the 1990 race, would think first about Ann Richards and female gender roles. And yet the public playing out of Williams' masculinity—was he a gentleman? A tough cowboy? A "good man," a "real man," or neither?—and individual voters' response to that unfolding became fully as significant to the race as were judgments about Ann Richards' "femininity." (Clayton Williams had said during the primary campaign season that he would not be comfortable running against a woman. As it turned out, his worries were prophetic.)

Of course, Deaux and Major would not think of a gubernatorial campaign as a test of their model of gendered perceptions because they mean to apply it to face-to-face encounters occurring in pairs or, at the most, in small groups. We, however, would like to suggest that campaigns *should* be thought of as an endlessly iterated series of such encounters, especially when the question at hand is one of voters' evaluations of candidates. The political context and the singularity of female seekers of high office provide the salience and the urgency predicting, in the Deaux and Major model, a strong and immediate invocation of gender role belief systems. The woman candidate's—the "target's"—self-presentation and self-verification can be seen first in her decision to run, and then in the degree to which she does or does not emphasize sex and gender. Although Deaux and Major do not make causal claims for their model, we could say that the ultimate causal effect (even though it is terribly difficult cleanly to separate from other considerations such as partisanship or issue position) would be the voters'—the "perceivers'"—choice. The final result of this web of interactions is that a woman is or is not elected to office.

We already know, for example, that voters construct their

Claytie and the Lady

candidate evaluations out of fairly complex, interactive "running tally" images encompassing far more than candidate issue positions (see Lodge, McGraw, and Stroh 1989), and that sex and gender stereotypes provide voters, inadvertently or not, with strong cues about what a candidate must be "like" (Alexander and Andersen 1991; Huddy and Terkildsen 1993), whether those cues come from the visual identification of female sex (Bowman 1984) or merely a female name (Sapiro 1982). These variable cues, responses, and adjustments stimulated by gender orientations—almost always going on in all social interactions between men and women—are especially intricate when the context is not a mere social exchange but an election, the choosing of a political leader, and are made even more tricky by the fact that "political leadership" *itself* has been gendered.

We can draw some evidence of this latter problem by comparing exit poll results from the Texas and California gubernatorial elections in 1990 and the California senate races in 1992. Dianne Feinstein was the Democratic candidate for governor of California while Ann Richards was campaigning in Texas. Feinstein lost by an even closer margin—less than one percent of the vote—than that by which Richards narrowly won. In 1992, Feinstein and Rep. Barbara Boxer were the two Democratic candidates for the U.S. Senate, in a very unusual election, given that both California's senate seats were up for grabs, both the nominees of one of the parties were women, and both women won election to the Senate. In the two 1990 gubernatorial races, voters were asked whether the sex of the candidate was "the single most important factor," "one of several important factors," or "not important" to the vote choice. Only tiny numbers of voters admitted that sex was *the* most important factor: 3.5% admitted this in Texas, and 4.1% did so in California. Among Texans, 14.5% would even consider the sex of the candidate "one of several important factors"; a comparable 17.3% of Californians chose this response. The overwhelming majorities in both places—82% in Texas and 78.6% in California, said that sex was *not* important to their choice of Governor.

And yet Feinstein's sex was always an issue in the campaign, as it was for Richards. In 1992, Feinstein was a stronger and wiser candidate, having learned from her experiences in 1990, but she was otherwise the same woman. She herself argued that, without intending to discriminate, voters were simply not "ready" for a woman Governor of California, but would accept a woman Senator, since legislative responsibilities were more consonant with women's traditional roles (Tolleson Rinehart 1994). Poll numbers may bear her out, although a change in the wording of the exit-poll responses makes it impossible for us to be certain: "single most important" in 1990 was changed to the easier to choose "very important" in 1992, and "one of several important factors" was relaxed to "somewhat important." Nonetheless, in the 1992 California Senate races, the most stringent category was chosen by a much, much larger 41.2% of voters, with another 34% saying that candidate sex was "somewhat important." In other words, *ten times* as many voters were willing to say that the sex of the candidate was a decisive factor in a senatorial election as had said so in the gubernatorial elections only two years earlier. Even with changes in the wording of response categories, that is an enormous increase. The candidates themselves, as Feinstein indicated, were also sensitive to gendered differences in perceptions of chief executive and legislative roles, and to the degree of women's acceptability in both. In 1990, neither Richards nor Feinstein made direct appeals on the basis of sex, and both were careful to avoid seeming to be the "women's candidate." In 1992, both Feinstein and Boxer frankly, and successfully, made appeals as and to women (Morris 1992; Tolleson Rinehart 1994; all figures computed by the authors from Voter Research and Surveys General Election Exit Polls State Files, 1990 and 1992).

Democratic media consultant Mark McKinnon understood implicitly that Ann Richards was seen, sometimes blurrily, through this welter of gendered perceptions, and that they would have to be taken into account as she was presented to voters:

> Ann was a breakthrough. I mean, we had to constantly fight this notion that, "Oh, well, yeah, sure she was Treasurer, but Governor is different." . . . [W]hat I think happens in any chief executive office

*election, when we elect Governors or Presidents,
what we are really electing is the head of a family
. . . We communicated that Ann Richards had to
make it on her own for a long time. That she was
matriarch and patriarch. Because she survived
tough times and the whole alcohol thing is a part of
that. You know she fought some tough battles and
won. And so everybody could be comfortable
because this woman had been through hell and
back and could do it again if she had to. You know,
she could take us there and protect us . . . and that
could be personified as the head of the family.
(Interview, 14 May 1991)*

When skilled campaign consultants construct these analyses, it is because they know (although perhaps not in the language of social psychology) that, indeed, a voter's candidate evaluation emerges in the context of individual, "face-to-face" interactions. They are highly contrived, of course: they are almost never *truly* face-to-face, since, in contemporary American politics, almost all voter-candidate "interaction" occurs via television news and paid campaign advertisements. They are not as continuously interactive, subject to response and adjustment, as are intimate social situations. But we might say that modern campaigns' polling and use of "focus groups" are attempts to check "perceivers'" actions, such that "targets" (candidates) can accordingly adjust their behavior. The candidate must *broadcast* her images: even if she directs different emphases to different likely constituencies—and she will—she is nonetheless trying to present an intimate picture of herself, but is doing so en masse.

In this chapter, then, as we view the election from the perspectives of Democratic and, to a lesser extent, Republican campaign experts, we should keep the contextual, interactive model of gendered behavior firmly in mind. First we offer campaign elites' retrospective assessments of campaign organization and strategy. We discuss the perennial problem of American politics—money—and the contemporary reason for that problem—television. Always in these discussions, we wish to ask how each campaign, but especially that of

Richards, was constructed to appeal to strengths while minimizing "negatives." What does the experience of passing through the Texas crucible say for other women who seek high office? Might the Richards case even offer some lessons for the first female major party candidate for President? In terms of the "political uses of symbolic women" (Sapiro 1993), it certainly will. Her campaign in 1990, we think, was a stone dropped into the pool of women's candidacies; the ripples were still spreading two years later. Richards' *1990* success helped make *1992* the "Year of the Woman," to the extent that it was that at all (for discussion of the Richards campaign's "spillover effects" on the 1992 California senatorial races, see Tolleson Rinehart 1994). This chapter also provides the analytical framework from which to understand the day-to-day events of the campaign presented in the next chapter. Those events are easier to interpret when our framework and the analytical strategies of the campaigns are kept in mind. Campaign operatives, of course, were even closer observers than we were, and the adequacy of their analyses was measured not merely by statistical significance but by a real outcome. Thus, we turn to their reflections.

CAMPAIGN OPERATIVES' PERSPECTIVES

The Williams campaign was quite well run during the Republican primary cycle, and extremely well funded, buoyed by nearly six million dollars from the candidate's personal fortune. Of the approximately twenty-two million dollars that Williams eventually spent on the primary and general elections combined, about eight and a half million dollars, or about 39%, came from his own pocket. More important, though, is the fact that Williams required little additional money during the primary, financing more than two-thirds of its costs (almost six million of approximately nine million dollars) himself (these and all figures for Williams' campaign expenditures are drawn from the *Dallas Morning News* data base of financial reports filed with the Secretary of State's office, courtesy of Austin bureau chief, Wayne Slater). All experts and observers agree that his personal wealth was

Claytie and the Lady

essential to his surprising, and commanding, victory in the Republican primary. The early, and seemingly unlimited, financial resources that he could provide his own candidacy were a gift that any candidate would give much to have. His primary campaign began early, and was exceptionally successful in its media use. As Milton Rister, his long-time associate and the first paid campaign staffer, told us,

> We started the cycle a lot earlier than the other [GOP candidates], in the fall, and from the time [Williams' most popular and award-winning advertisement, in which he stands before a staged chain gang and tells viewers that he will teach drug users "the joys of bustin' rocks"] went on, we moved one point a day against [early favorite and former Congressman Kent Hance] . . . And that's what made him a viable candidate. Those deep pockets carried him through . . . The ability to put [the ad] up on TV, to get saturation across the state, was important, and that's where Claytie's money came in. But a bad ad wouldn't have worked. The public relations firm who had worked with him in Clay Desta [Communications—a long-distance telephone provider and one of Williams' many business ventures] was able to "capture the spirit" . . . (Interview, 3 August 1993)

Williams sailed easily to victory in the Republican primary, even though he had already begun to make the kinds of utterances that would eventually bring him down to a legendary defeat. Who was he, and why had he run? He had no previous political experience, but both his father and grandfather, whose lives he always aspired to live up to, had had political ambitions. And Claytie had apparently enjoyed the public spotlight he drew to himself when he starred in his own advertisements for ClayDesta Communications (often sitting by a campfire in cowboy garb), and equally visibly lobbied for changes in communications regulations (by, for example, riding his horse up the steps of the Capitol building in Austin, before obliging television news crews).

Williams is the grandson and son of wealthy ranchers near Fort Stockton in West Texas, a graduate of Texas A&M University, and a man who, in less than two decades, had turned speculative oil leases into a personal conglomerate of oil-drilling contracting, ranching, banking, and communications. He seems to be quite conservative politically, but a sophisticated political ideology was never much in evidence during the campaign. On Claytie's entry into the gubernatorial race, Milton Rister says, "We all started by thinking, 'We'll have a good time, but we're not going to win.' When 'Bustin' Rocks' hit, we knew he'd be a viable candidate. He was having a ball, a real good time. All that changed with the plane crash [in February 1990, when one of Williams' planes, carrying his three closest friends and business associates, crashed, killing all aboard] . . . He never was the same after the plane crash . . . " (interview, 3 August 1993). But by the time of the plane crash, he was already deemed unstoppable, the GOP's nominee-designate for Governor of Texas.

His campaign organization, so effective in the primary, remained flush with funds in the general election, but it was no longer well run. Rister told us that the people who had designed the tremendously effective television advertisements in the primary had no creative control in the general election. Indeed, in one case, when the campaign wanted to portray Williams as exceptionally businesslike in an ad about state government spending that turned out to have featured inaccurate figures, the ad had to be pulled, corrected, and re-run, but not without attracting notice even from Republicans (Jamieson 1992: 159; the Richards campaign was also forced to pull one misleading ad). "Claytie's" campaign organization was most seriously hampered by Claytie himself, as the candidate acknowledged when, after the election, he said that he had shot himself in the foot. No one would disagree. If responsibility for his defeat could be assigned to a single source, it would be that of his own extremely controversial statements, beginning with his quip to reporters in March, during a rainy outing on his ranch, that "the weather's like rape. If it's inevitable, you might as well lie back and enjoy it." Milton Rister (interview, 3 August 1993) said about the "rape joke" incident that "people don't understand that that's just the way he was raised, raised to be a gentleman, to treat women as different, as special. Instead of seeing that, they saw the rape joke, and . . . we made a major mistake . . . You know, don't ever step on your opponent's bad press. Ann Richards and Jim Mattox had each other by the throat [in the Democratic primary] and instead of letting that happen, we . . ." (Here Rister trailed off. Rister, like Williams, does not seem to appreciate that reaction to the "joke" was based not on the fact that he told it before reporters, but on the fact that he would *think* of telling it. Many women felt that Williams—and, by extension, the Republicans—didn't "get it.")

The major failure of his campaign organization, many felt, was in not keeping him "managed" enough to avoid making such mistakes. Karl Rove, Republican campaign consultant, believes that it could and should be considered such a failure:

> [I]t just goes to show that a lot of money hides a lot of structural problems . . . I do think that he became repetitious. He had no additional message by the fall. And the two times that they tried to establish a new message, [they failed to do so] . . . there were lots of us who said, "Why do you let the guy, after you've kept the guy in a cocoon for a year and done so successfully, let him out the last two weeks of the campaign?" . . . frankly I think more important than the gender-based items, which were important, I don't want to disregard that, more important than those, though, were in the final week, there were three things, all of them occurring in the last month of the campaign and two of them within the last two weeks . . . When Clayton Williams refused to shake [Richards'] hand he looked bitter, beat, and small . . . When he goes on the television in the final week of the campaign and says, "I don't know what that [constitutional] amendment [on the ballot] was, Modesta [Williams' wife] told me how to vote on it" [the amendment altered the Governor's state agency appointment powers] . . . it looks stupid and not managerial and not the tough guy, business guy

> *in control. That hurt him. And then when he said,*
> *"I haven't paid income tax" [when it emerged that*
> *in 1986 the millionaire had been able to use the tax*
> *code to avoid all tax liability] . . . (Here Rove trailed*
> *off; interview, 14 October 1991)*

Rove's argument is that these three "October surprises" (they are described in more detail in the next chapter) that all agree were terribly damaging to Williams were preventable, had the campaign staff only worked harder to control their candidate.

Rove minimizes the effects of gender-role perceptions on voters' judgments about these mistakes (nor would we want to overstate them). His Republican colleagues David Weeks, a media consultant (but not with the Williams campaign), Royal Masset, the Research Director of the Texas Republican party, and Milton Rister, Williams' associate, make more allowances for these mistakes being interpretable in gendered terms. Rister says, "The development of the cowboy, tough image was a bad mistake. It embedded the idea that Claytie was part of the chauvinist West Texas culture." Masset argues that Williams tried to present the "ranch foreman" or "frontiersman" model of leadership that may have worked in Texas in the past, but does not work today. "[F]rankly," he says, "women aren't going to fake being a foreman," but can much more successfully enter the new managerial, "cognitive" leadership profile. But, with that said, Ann Richards also presented some aspects of the populist "frontierswoman," but in her case successfully and to her advantage (emphasis added; Masset interview, 13 May 1991). Weeks, whose business is the presentation of images, and who was working on two other statewide office campaigns while the gubernatorial story unfolded, was more likely to stress the kinds of (sometimes inchoate) dynamics that the Deaux and Major model would seek to examine:

> *In my experience it is very difficult to run against a*
> *woman unless she is an incumbent with a record . . .*
> *A female candidate can "get away with" more . . .*
> *I have handled women and I encourage it . . . A*

woman can be a little more liberal than a man and
[still] be accepted by conservatives . . . This sexual
harassment concept [referring to the Hill-Thomas
hearings] is going to move into the political process.
I think it is going to become even more difficult for
men to attack a woman . . . Clayton Williams was
losing ground with . . . the [Republican] women
[and they] would be looking for a place to go on the
ballot, and so we really tried to fill that void for the
Republican party [with his two candidates, one of
whom was Kay Bailey Hutchison, elected to fill the
State Treasurer's office that Richards had left
vacant] . . . To be fair to Ann, she stayed in the race.
There were some things that she could have done
that no matter what Williams had done he would
have won. But she didn't. She stayed in the race.
She countered the way she should have countered.
She did all the right things from the perspective of
how you go about running against a man. She got a
little more aggressive than I would have thought.
But it is okay, a woman can be aggressive against a
man, especially if she is already an aggressive
woman . . . They [many Republican women] were
just sick of Clayton Williams. They tried to support
him. They tried to stay with him . . . But because
of his "foot-in-the-mouth," it was too embarrassing.
It just finally got to the point where they said, "I
just can't tolerate this man anymore." Women will
react that way. They are a lot faster to react than
men are . . . Their antennae are a lot keener . . .
(Interview, 14 May 1991)

For Weeks, it is clear, campaign strategy must take the dominant gender-role orientations of the culture into account. In
particular, while women have had a difficult time winning
high political office, they may now be able to take advantage
of both "modern" and "traditional" gender role beliefs. "Modern" roles make them acceptable as candidates, and "traditional" roles make them harder to attack by male opponents.
Weeks said:

*I know the Richards campaign had to be played
completely different. And I don't blame them. I
think Ann's position improved when Clayton made
mistakes. Of course, that is the whole idea behind a
campaign, the campaign is won by the person who
makes the fewest mistakes. And she made fewer
mistakes than he did. That is a classic case. But I
have never seen, and I have been doing this for
twenty years, I have never seen anybody that had
the lead and had the support of the people like he
did lose it over a six-month period. I mean, he gave
that race away.*

It is possible that Williams could have "given that race away"
had he been facing a male opponent; most observers agree
that the personality and image displayed in the campaign were
the genuine Clayton Williams, and he would thus have presented many of the same strengths and weaknesses regardless of the sex of his opponent—nor, in that case, could he
have been very easily "managed" into someone else, despite
Karl Rove's insistence otherwise. The difficulty is that no
one *could* fail to pay regard to Ann Richards' sex, and many
of Williams' actions as well as numerous Williams-Richards
interactions were refracted through the prisms of gender in
ways that could only fail to be confronted by someone will-
fully ignoring gender. Even the informational mistakes that
cost him his image as a "tough, in-control guy" were magni-
fied by gender orientations. "Toughness" is "masculine" (as
well as "gubernatorial"), and Ann Richards, because she was
"tougher" and more competent, looked more "masculine"
than Williams in some ways.

The Richards campaign, in contrast to that of Williams
but similar to those of other women candidates, was chroni-
cally underfunded, especially through the long primary and
runoff season and the summer. It was charged with being
overdependent, in the view of some politicos, on volunteers,
and it experienced some tension between the "professionals" and the "amateurs" who ran it. The "professionals" were
unquestionably just that: some of the best-known Texan and
national Democratic campaign consultants worked for

Richards. "Amateur," however, is a bit of a misnomer. While most of the highest-placed campaign officials had never run such a large campaign, or for such an important office, they were hardly strangers to Texas politics. And, while they acknowledge that some mistakes were made, they also point out that the failure of traditional "big donors" to get on the Richards bandwagon meant that volunteers (and small donors) *had* to be relied upon (see the discussion of money in the next section of this chapter); they and the professionals also agree that an early campaign game plan was developed, and hewed to. We have heard from Republicans; now the Democrats get their chance. Democratic consultant George Shipley says:

> [W]omen who run for office in Texas tend to be products of a very, very crude political system. And they tend to be, therefore, [people who have] the stronger wills before they ever get to the arena . . . The negative poses a particularly unusual set of circumstances for the woman candidate. At the same time, the female is generally able to resist negative attacks more effectively. Simply by virtue of the tactical position of her gender. The male who attacks the female, no matter how mild the issue disagreements might be, runs the risk of being perceived as "slapping a lady," so it has to be done very carefully . . . It always takes two in the ritual. And what we did, we made Clayton lose it. We were statistically unelectable. We went in [from the very bitter primary, when Jim Mattox accused Richards of drug use and she implied that former Governor Mark White had inappropriately profited from his office] with all these negatives . . . The Governor was unprepared for the depth of animosity she received in the primary at the hands of Jim Mattox . . . And critics said that she was unelectable after that, that she had essentially lost her political arms and legs after the Mattox accusations . . . What happened to Ann is a beautiful story. When you go through these experiences you either tend to come

*apart and stay apart or you draw strength from
them. And what she did, by Labor Day she drew
mental strength from the primary bashing . . . We
concluded that Williams had created an artifice of
an image which was at variance with who this guy
really was and we needed to pull him out from
behind the commercials . . . We had to make the
campaign become more than just a siege. You know,
my catapult versus your catapult . . . We had to
make it more like a game of rugby or Australian
football . . . and we had to get the fellow out there
and then pitch him the ball and let it flow. So that
he just can't go make another commercial and
campaign like the proverbial knight in the castle.
And if a campaign flows like that, then people get
interested. And so we started pitching pretty hard.
(Interview, 14 May 1991)*

Mary Beth Rogers, not a campaign "professional" but neither was she an amateur, lamented not only the pain of the
primary season, but also the frustrations associated with being accused of running a poor campaign.[1] Everyone, it seemed,
could have done the job better:

*[W]e had had a terrible summer. I had come in in
May, the primary was so difficult, so bitter, everybody was so demoralized, and we had to rebuild an
entire campaign structure. In a rebuilding process
there is a certain amount of disorganization and
confusion, and that went on during the summer. But
it was the groundwork for what had to be done, and
not much of it was visible. So we continued to have
to fight that perception [that the campaign was
ineffective] . . . We had a strategy, and our polling
was going to help us measure its success, we knew
we were twenty-four points down, behind Clayton
Williams, at the beginning of the summer. And we
had a strategy to decrease that point spread so that
by the first of October, we would be only ten points
down. Now, that doesn't sound like a lot . . . [but]*

> *we knew that if we were within ten points, we had a*
> *shot at winning the election . . . When you say that*
> *to somebody, and all they see is you being hit on the*
> *head, day after day, Clayton Williams with his TV,*
> *they don't believe you. They think you're crazy. And*
> *yet the campaign was not being run by novices . . . I*
> *had a* New York Times *reporter [call in the spring of*
> *1991, during the first months of the Richards ad-*
> *ministration, with questions about the state budget*
> *deficit; he greeted Rogers' optimism skeptically] and*
> *he said, "Well, I'm not as optimistic as you are, but*
> *then I didn't believe you during the campaign*
> *either." And I said, "Well, when are you guys gonna*
> *learn?" (Interview, 15 October 1991)*

Whether amateur or professional, Democrat or Republican, all the people we talked to are in striking agreement on
their analysis of the campaign, although of course the Republicans place more blame on Clayton Williams for making
mistakes, and the Democrats take more credit for having
forced him to make them. Most of their conclusions match
our own, based on our observation, and are bolstered by the
account of key campaign events in the next chapter, as well
as by findings from exit-poll research presented in Chapter 5.

MONEY

Aside from gender's significance in other factors, such as increasing Republican identification in Texas politics and the
moralistic, traditional nature of Texas political culture, it
played yet another important role. It affected fundraising.
Attorney and Richards campaign fundraiser Martha Smiley
and Richards' son-in-law and deputy campaign manager Kirk
Adams both told us that although Richards was a "star" after
the 1988 Democratic Nominating Convention and had favorably impressed the banking community with her actions
as State Treasurer, traditional large donors to Democratic
campaigns would not contribute in the early days and, after a
vicious primary and runoff season, were reluctant to

**TABLE 3.1. Time and Size of Contributions to the
Richards Campaign, in Numbers of Donors**

Year of last contribution:	1988	1989	1990	Total
Highest contribution				
< $100	2,798	2,378	15,985	21,161
$100–$249	556	603	5,600	6,759
$250–$499	178	111	1,050	1,339
$500–$999	136	105	970	1,211
$1,000–$4,999	157	99	1,301	1,557
$5,000–$9,999	12	9	234	255
> $9,999	4	2	146	152

Source: Jennifer Treat, Finance Director, Richards for Governor Campaign.

contribute during the general campaign because they feared she couldn't win (interviews, 13 May 1991 and 14 August 1991, respectively). Smiley says that she cannot document it, but she is convinced that many donors simply were not going to give money to a woman. Adams says that, recognizing these problems from the beginning, the campaign knew it would have to rely on small donors. Indeed, small donors flocked to Richards and made some 33,000 donations at levels below the hundred-dollar range, as can also be seen in Table 3.1. In fact, though the campaign got off to a painful and exasperating start, Richards' *success* as a fundraiser created something of a turning point in the financial fortunes of credible women candidates for high office. We believe, as does EMILY's List (a Democratic group that "bundles" contributions *for* women candidates *from* women), that Richards' success in 1990 greatly aided women Senate candidates in 1992 (Griffith 1993).

Women made up a substantial proportion of the "small" donors (as with other campaigns, here, too, large numbers of women have not yet had the experience or resources to become "big" donors, but that state of affairs is rapidly changing). Some women gave much more: Smiley told us of a loan from a businesswoman of $50,000 that the campaign dreaded losing, and an East Texas woman on Social Security who actually took out a loan *herself* in order to give money to Ann

Richards (when the campaign staff realized what she had done, they beseeched her to stop). But although the campaign operatives found it a strain to have to rely so heavily on small donors, they also knew they were accomplishing something quite new for women. Campaign finance director Jennifer Treat says:

> [P]eople who write checks to women candidates do so regardless of, it's not a partisan thing, it's, "She's the woman in the race. It doesn't matter to me whether it's August of '89 or April of '90, I'm going to start supporting her now and I'll support her throughout," whereas most contributors are either partisan or ideological, and the outcome of the primary plays a role in their decision to be aboard politically. So we went about identifying sources of income for Ann, and some of these would never have been available, probably, to a male candidate in the same situation. One of these was, of course, EMILY's List. After some brief period of negotiation they decided to endorse her, they mailed very early for Ann [soliciting donations], and were responsible for putting close to $200,000 into the primary election . . . (Interview, 15 October 1991)

Treat also developed a novel, but very labor-intensive, strategy called "Ann TV," meant, obviously, to attract money specifically for purchases of television time. The strategy required persuading a small number of women to become "Executive Producers" who would then take responsibility for enlisting larger numbers of women as "Network Executives." The strategy realized close to a half million dollars, but Treat believes that its "high-maintenance" (or time-consuming) nature prevented it from netting more. And more was always needed, for modern campaigns in places the size of Texas are almost addictively dependent on effective television advertisements.

Another example of the differences between the Richards and Williams campaigns lies in their "donor pyramids." As Table 3.1 illustrates, Richards' donors form an inverted pyramid, with more than ten times as many small donors as large ones. While the Richards organization was top heavy with small donors, but with the number of larger donors increasing as time went on, in the Williams camp it was just the reverse. According to his February 1990 report to the Secretary of State, during the primary, Williams had raised $1.3 million from 151 separate contributions, and $2 million from 271 contributions, for an *average* donation of about $7,000. According to his report for the period of March to July, he had raised $4 million from 1,277 separate contributions, dropping the average donation to $3,000. By the end of the general election reporting period, the average contribution had dropped to $214 (figures courtesy of Wayne Slater). Clearly, Williams' own early money made his nomination possible, after which traditional Republican donors came aboard. In Richards' case, it was her primary success that began to make money available to her in the general election—much the harder way to have to do it.

TELEVISION

Fundraising problems meant that those running the Richards campaign knew they could do little in the way of television advertising until the late summer and fall. They assumed that the campaign would remain underfunded relative to the Williams campaign, and that assumption turned out to be correct. Kirk Adams and others noted that the campaign was criticized for not being more "active" before the fall, but said that they were sticking to their game plan, shepherding their financial resources. In fact, the bulk of the Richards campaign commercials were produced and aired from mid-September to election day. Although financial exigency may have dictated the schedule, they were probably more effective at this late point because media coverage of Williams' gaffes had had a chance by then to create a backlash effect helpful to Richards. (Certainly, something similar had happened during the primary, when an ad run by Richards' opponent, Jim Mattox, strongly accusing Richards of having used drugs *as an officeholder* "sworn to uphold the law" caused a seven-

point drop in the polls not for Richards, but for Mattox;
Jamieson 1992: 115).

As Richards' advertisements were becoming more effective, Williams' were becoming much less so. Milton Rister
says, "A big mistake on our part: instead of staying negative
[on Richards, late in the campaign], we went up with something warm and fuzzy. And it didn't define Claytie or reduce
his negatives, and it didn't raise hers. We could have come
on with a negative drug ad, but Claytie said no, because he
respected her for conquering her alcoholism . . ." (interview,
3 August 1993). Rister told us that there had been damaging
evidence against Richards, and attributed the lack of an ad to
Williams' chivalry, as you see. On the other hand, the conventional wisdom floating about at the time was that any
"evidence" of drug use that the Williams campaign obtained
was probably obtained from her Democratic foe, Jim Mattox.
And yet Mattox's "evidence" was never publicly substanti-
ated or corroborated.

Gender also very significantly affected the way candidate
Richards was presented in advertisements. Adams,
McKinnon, Shipley, Ivins, and Masset all agree with the most
recent scholarly literature that finds that women candidates
can use their sex as an advantage *not* by making too-obvious
appeals to virtual representation, but by capitalizing on the
issues and leadership styles voters assume women offer.
Women can, for example, be presented as the "change candidate," for reform, good government, and careful stewardship
of taxpayer dollars (though some of the 1992 Senate races
may call for a reassessment of this assumption, at least in
the short run, as with our view of the California races).
Women can capitalize on the "compassion issues" of community health and well-being. Women are seen as less cor-
rupt and more accountable; Richards' autumn campaign commercials were directed toward this bent, portraying Richards
as the capable and accountable executive (although Republican media consultant David Weeks thought these ads failed
to show enough of her "warm, feminine" side), and empha-
sizing her pledge to bring about insurance reforms and changes
in hazardous waste management, among other issues.

The Richards campaign was criticized by some feminists for its reluctance to emphasize particular women's issues. Although Richards is adamantly pro-choice on abortion, only one campaign commercial, featuring *Designing Women* actress Annie Potts, dealt with the issue, and other feminist questions were only subtly addressed. But Kirk Adams and Jane Hickie both say that this was deliberate: the campaign knew of feminists' impassioned support for Richards, "monitored it constantly," and did not want to "preach to the choir" at the expense of reaching out to other groups. George Shipley and Mark McKinnon both feel very strongly that this—avoidance of direct appeals on the basis of sex—was the only way Richards could make her sex and voters' gendered perceptions work for her. They also insist that women must not appear to be too far from the traditional trappings of femininity and "traditional family values." Recall McKinnon's claim that voters are looking for "the head of a family": in this case, a matriarch rather than a patriarch was chosen, but in part because Richards *did* look like a matriarch (she has "great Republican hair," Molly Ivins says), and not someone who was "extreme" or "out of touch" in lifestyle.

Professionals and amateurs in the campaign consistently worried about striking the best balance of "appropriate" femininity, probity, and toughness. Toughness, contrary to what may be assumed, was not the problem: Richards *is* tough—she can be quite intimidating—and effective. And her survival of the primary campaign had shown her as well as the voters just how strong she was. The difficulty was in showing her warmth, her "feminine" side. Shipley and Adams point out that national media consultant Robert Squiers worked hard to develop a commercial featuring Ann and her father (her "Daddy") Cecil Willis, simply to reassure voters that Richards *did* have a traditional family and "traditional family values"—that she had not sprung from "the belly of the beast," as George Shipley put it. The image problem resulted not only from Ann's genuine toughness but also, as Molly Ivins insists, the fact that she is good-looking and possesses a razor-sharp wit, both qualities that would be unambiguously valued in a man but can be threatening in a woman.

Claytie and the Lady

INTO THE TEXAS POLITICAL CRUCIBLE

Charges that Ann Richards had used illegal drugs had dogged her throughout the primary and general election campaigns, as we have seen. But from the time that her primary opponent, Jim Mattox, raised the issue until election day, her campaign stuck by Richards' decision not to answer questions. This was in part Richards' own insistence, as a recovering alcoholic whose battle against alcohol had become well known, that an answer would only lead to more questions, and that answering the continuing questions about drug use would deter substance-abusers from getting help.[2] But gender played a role, too: as Kirk Adams pointed out, the long-time politician and successful candidate for Lieutenant Governor, Bob Bullock, was also a recovering alcoholic, and the question of other drug use was never an issue in his campaign. And, as George Shipley maintains, while a man's confession to marital infidelity or drug use may well be seen as strength of character, similar questions about a woman virtually irremediably tar her with the stain of "unwomanly," and certainly "unladylike," behavior. Voters are still shocked by and unforgiving of behavior in a woman that they will accept in a man. Hence the conclusion of Richards and her campaign that she had no choice but to "take the pounding." And finally, lack of evidence substantiating the charges as well as some backlash of sympathy for her and against her opponents meant that the drug-use issue, if it did not positively help Richards, at least did not permanently hurt her.

But gender-role issues never faded and, oddly, most agree that Williams, not Richards, was the one to make an issue of them. Recall Royal Masset's discussion of the past Texas model of political leader as ranch foreman, "bashing people around." Williams certainly presented that image of himself—he was the hardhitting, freewheeling oilman and rancher who would "make Texas great again." His colorful commercials portrayed him teaching drug users the "joys of bustin' rocks." His image was one of *literally* riding his horse into the sunset. If Williams is, in fact, a real leader, any chance to crystallize that image in voters' minds was lost in the furor over his constant verbal gaffes, almost all of which emerged directly from controversial views of gender roles and of women.

Journalist Molly Ivins and the Richards campaign team all believed—correctly in the event—that Williams' behavior would alienate not only large numbers of women, but large numbers of sophisticated urban Republican voters as well. Those involved in the Richards campaign, believing Williams to be vulnerable in this regard, pushed, particularly in the autumn, not only to reinforce Williams' mistakes (in a commercial called "Clayton Williams in his own words") but to question just how close to the law Williams had sailed in some of his freewheeling business activities (in commercials called "Meet Clayton Williams"). Ivins pointed out that Williams had become an "embarrassment, gauche, crude" in the eyes of many Texans. In fact, at the election's end, usually staunchly Republican Dallas County had gone for Richards (Flick 1990). Claytie, as we have said, might have been just as "macho" facing a male opponent, but against Richards, his machismo finally backfired.

I think . . . that another thing that men find very threatening is funny women. I mean, with Ann it was a real problem. Funny and good-looking. And female. . . if you can find the comments right after her convention speech [the keynote address at the 1988 Democratic Nominating Convention], there are some really funny ones. They just did not know what to make of her. I think funny women are perceived as [castrating]. If they realize that a woman can be funny, I think men are afraid that that tone can be used against them. And they don't like it.

—MOLLY IVINS, interview with the authors, 14 May 1991

CHAPTER 4

The Unfolding of a Gubernatorial Campaign

When Ann Richards declared her candidacy for Governor, many people expected (with varying degrees of pleasure or dismay) that they *would* see the funny (or sharp-tongued) woman that the whole nation had come to feel it knew. There was to be little laughter in the campaign, though. From the beginning of the primary season until election day in November, as Mary Beth Rogers told us, the Richards campaign felt it "had to come in every day girded up for war." Missing her humor, and the fun it would add to the race, many said "let Ann be Ann," but this business of winning the Governor's Mansion started seriously and became increasingly grim.

The Democratic primary featured three contestants. Two of them, Richards and former Member of Congress and incumbent Attorney General Jim Mattox, were from the Progressive wing of the party. The remaining candidate, former Governor Mark White, is a moderate with, most would say, a considerably less vivid personality than that of Richards or Mattox, and often thought of as being tough to the point of meanness, despite his long record of compassionate public service. Most observers felt that the real race would be between the two liberals, Mattox and Richards. And despite the fact that this was the *Democratic* primary, with two *liberals* leading in the polls, discussion of Progressive public policy almost always took a back seat to the usual Texas politics of personalities and ornery cultural conservatism—at one point, for example, the three candidates appeared to be so eager to outdo one another in support for the death penalty that they became the subject of a sketch on the television program *Saturday Night Live*, with impersonators of the three candidates each dressed as the Grim Reaper (Ivins 1991). Beneath the spectacle lay genuinely Progressive policy agendas, especially on the part of Richards and Mattox. But the primary is best remembered for its terribly bitter and negative personal tone. Of Richards' two Democratic primary opponents, Jim Mattox savaged her early and often with charges that she had abused not only alcohol but numerous other drugs. She, in turn, made a breathtakingly negative surgical strike against her other primary opponent, former Governor Mark White. As we will see in the coming pages, Mattox's attacks against her finally worked to her benefit, but her own attacks on White (who never forgave her and would not campaign for her in the general election) did not leave a good taste in voters' mouths. She survived the primary still standing, but bloodied, and far down in the polls. Meanwhile, as we saw in the last chapter, the Republican primary was a far tamer affair, with Clayton Williams surging past much more experienced but less well-funded and colorful Republicans such as West Texan Kent Hance and lawyer Tom Luce, the latter now best known as a close adviser to Ross Perot.

The general election campaign against Clayton Williams provided humor, but because of Williams' words and actions, and not because Ann Richards' funny, razor-witted side was often in evidence. The campaign, for all the surprising events in it, remained a war. And warring is not something women traditionally are supposed to do (although they do it more often than is recognized; for reflections on the woman warrior, see Elshtain 1987; Fraser 1990). Richards had to be tough, she had to be "warm and feminine," she had to be competent and accessible. In order to win, she had to be a political warrior. How would that be seen through the prisms of gender?

1924 REDUX

Just as "Jane Y" McCallum and, oddly enough, Miriam "Ma" Ferguson had scaled the heights of politics during the great suffrage phase of the women's movement, Ann Richards emerged during the movement's reincarnation and transformation into contemporary feminism. Governor Richards has more in common with McCallum than she does with Ferguson, but there are some notable parallels in the contexts of the Richards and Ferguson elections. First, in the elections of both 1924 and 1990, personalities virtually overwhelmed issues in the conduct of the campaign. Second, both campaigns were unusually bitter and controversial. Third, both campaigns divided women sharply over questions not only of issues but also of gender ideologies. In the Richards-Williams campaign, men too were divided, but less closely (Gillman 1990). Fourth, in both campaigns the issue of a woman holding the state's highest political office, and what that would mean, was a powerful undercurrent, far more powerful than it ever was in the intervening years. McCallum and Ferguson illustrate contrasting gender-role ideologies among the women of the 1920s. Ann Richards' persona also signifies the contrast between traditional and "modern" or egalitarian roles. For men, the contrast may be a very serious matter of principle and belief. For women, it goes farther: the choice determines the shape of their lives.

In the election of 1924, Miriam Ferguson was never thought by anyone to be the person who would actually govern. The question was how much power Jim Ferguson would exercise, not *whether* he would exercise power. At the same time, patriarchal chivalry—and, on the distaff side, feminist scorn for the "slave wife"—accepted that Ma could not be held accountable for Jim. Voters and elites alike thus put themselves in the anomalous position of deliberately electing an official whom they would not hold to official accountability, simply because it was impossible for anyone from Jim to his most violent opponents to consider that Mrs. Ferguson could or should truly govern.

In the general election campaign of 1990, in contrast, it was equally impossible to believe that Ann Richards would *not* be her own woman, or that she would *not* exercise gubernatorial power to the fullest were she elected. She had been in the public eye as the State Treasurer since 1982, her keynote address at the 1988 Democratic National Nominating Convention had brought her international attention, and her character had been put on trial in a vicious primary battle.

She revealed much of herself and her past, including her divorce and her recovering alcoholism, in her 1989 autobiography, *Straight from the Heart.* Once Attorney General Jim Mattox began insinuating that she had used drugs other than alcohol, he and the press attacked her relentlessly throughout the spring, until she could not appear in any venue without "Did you use drugs?" being the first and often most frequently asked question. She, too, went on the attack, abandoning her commitment to positive campaigning in the desperate need to survive the primary. Her campaign organization believed that she had to disable Mark White in order to enter a runoff with Jim Mattox in a tenable position. And so the campaign began airing commercials that implied, without actually making the accusation, that White had improperly benefited from office. White's candidacy faded. But Richards emerged from the primary and subsequent runoff election—where she handily defeated Mattox—shaken, with "high negatives" among the voting public (Swartz 1990). This had not been some gentle ideal of a "woman's" campaign style. It had been vintage Texas politics, red in tooth and claw.[1]

Clayton Williams had had a much easier time of it in the Republican primary; while his infamous "if rape is inevitable, lie back and enjoy it" comment in March had created a furor in the press—and among many women—there was also considerable sentiment for "understanding that that's just Claytie," that rough, salty language is a part of the cowboy myth. As Republican consultant Karl Rove pointed out, the "[poll] numbers didn't move" immediately after the rape remark. Voters' dispositions did not appear to shift until quite late in the campaign, after a long, dense accumulation of Williams gaffes had worn voter tolerance of him away.

PERSONALITY IS STILL THE ISSUE

Still, the gender differences in candidate affect had emerged seven months before the general election, as the figures in Table 4.1 make clear. In the aggregate, women demonstrated considerable ambivalence about both candidates, but men sharply preferred Williams to Richards. The harsh primary

TABLE 4.1. Voters' Favorable and Unfavorable Opinions of the Candidates, Spring 1990

Opinions	Men[*]		Women[†]	
	Richards %	*Williams* %	*Richards* %	*Williams* %
Favorable	37.1	52.8	41.4	34.4
Don't know	18.2	24.1	25.0	26.6
Unfavorable	44.6	23.1	33.9	39.1

Source: The Texas Poll, conducted by telephone 28 April–12 May. *N* of cases (618) includes only those registered voters who recognized both candidates. The marginal frequencies supplied were analyzed by the authors using the SAS-PC statistical software program. Percentages may not total 100 because of rounding.

[*]Differences significant at $p < .01$.

[†]No significant difference.

campaign and questions about Richards' private life had clearly taken their toll. In campaign consultant George Shipley's view, women win when they can adopt certain masculine characteristics *without* appearing to deviate from conventional expectations of femininity, or womanliness. A man's confession of drug use or marital infidelity can be turned into evidence of character strength, but admission by women of such an error is perceived as character weakness. Ann Richards never wavered in her refusal to answer questions about drug use, but the favorability ratings hint that the question still troubled voters, and that men were perhaps more disturbed by such questions.

It is difficult to argue that a male candidate emerging from the kind of primary battle that Richards endured would not also have looked tarnished. There is, however, no avoiding the singularity of her sex. Recall from Deaux and Major (1987) that gender schemata are especially quickly activated in contexts where there are many men but only one woman, and in contexts where gender is highly salient. We would argue that Richards' presence as the woman candidate in a field of men (at least two of whom—Mattox in the Democratic primary and Williams in the Republican primary—were not just men but "tough guys"), in a *particularly* gendered setting—the "male" world of politics—more than fulfills expectations that gender belief systems would be triggered, indeed would be firing wildly. Under these circumstances, it is no surprise that personalities would rapidly dominate issue positions.

Three of the campaign consultants we talked to offer interesting judgments on what transpired in the primary in this regard. One, Republican Karl Rove, minimizes gender. The other two, Republican David Weeks and Democrat George Shipley, see it as tremendously important not only to voters' perceptions but to the crafting of the campaign in the first place. The Republicans, of course, differ from the Democrat in their affective response to the primary (with Rove disgusted and Weeks grudgingly admiring). We will begin with the Democrat, George Shipley, on the gendered facets of the campaign:

> [A]s my 73-year-old mother likes to say, "A gentleman never asks and a lady never, never admits to anything" . . . And so psychology works in a negative campaign. The woman will simply walk the coals psychologically, and, as it were, take the pounding and emerge, often quite scarred up with high negatives . . . But the history of the Richards campaign, [although] you can't generalize with one campaign, is that the voters will accept those negatives and go on and reach second and third conclusions. Which is what happened. Now, the ritual of the negative campaign is a bit strained in that the woman has a hard time launching the first negative attack. In general, the better tactical position is to let the male figure do the attacking and then respond rhetorically as the outraged person who has been attacked personally.

So Ann Richards managed to survive Jim Mattox's attempt to savage her. But because she in turn went after Mark White, she could not end the primary as the noble "injured woman." Shipley continues:

> The "life value" argument . . . is so intrinsic and

*basic to the success of female campaigns that it has
to be understood. It is what Dick Wirthlin calls . . .
the "hope, earth, faith, smile, mother quotient." Ann
Richards' negatives were so high at various points,
we were constrained to make [the insurance reform
commercial featuring Richards walking arm-in-arm
with her elderly father, Cecil Willis] simply demonstrating that she had normal parents, that she was
not born out of the belly of the beast. And that she
had a mommy and a daddy. We don't have "fathers"
in Texas, we have "daddys." (Interview, 14 May 1991)*

Shipley called Richards' survival of the primary a "beau-
tiful story" because she was able to draw strength from it
rather than be broken by it. Karl Rove violently disagrees.

*I think that for the vast majority of people, both
Claytie's and Ann's behavior were not gender-based
decisions. They were based on their view of what the
Governor of the State of Texas should act like. And
they said on election day, "I don't think he acts like
one and I don't frankly think she acts like one, but I
got to make a decision and I'll give the call slightly to
her" . . . Remember, we had Ann Richards saying [in
the primary] that [former] Governor [Mark] White
was a crook. TV ads, where did he get that money to
buy a million-dollar house when he had that little
salary as Governor? Not one shred of truth, not one
bit of evidence. I [dislike Mark White] . . . But nobody deserves to have that kind of stuff said about
them. And she has been doing that for years . . . it
crosses the line from being tough to being vindictive
and mean . . . [Senator Alan] Simpson [R-Wyoming]
does it occasionally, but she did it a lot . . . And she
has this personality where if she is in Waco, by God,
she has the biggest twang you have ever heard in
your life. And if she is in North Dallas, she is not
country, she is cosmopolitan. And when she goes out
of the state, that twang comes back again because it
is fashionable . . . To me the story is not that she beat*

> *[Williams], it is how did he hang on until the last week of the campaign? . . . She was not that popular when she began and she was not that popular when it ended. It was that she wasn't him. (Interview, 14 October 1991)*

Republican media consultant David Weeks, on the other hand, thinks sex and gender play critical roles in the choices made about how to present women candidates. He, like political psychologists, assumes that voters now seek some measure of androgyny, of the combination of the "best" masculine and feminine characteristics.

> *Ann Richards was way too much on the masculine side. And I think that they didn't just soften her enough. And the reason that they didn't was because of that primary battle. She came away from that as being a cold-blooded executioner. It virtually, I would say, had she lost the general election I don't think she would have ever gotten elected again. She would have been dead politically. It took her all that time to get, from the primary to the general election, it took her all that time to get to the point to where she was acceptable . . . Even [though she won the primary], she won it against a candidate who was worse than she, Jim Mattox. I mean, that guy, just look at the data on him, and it is negative. But Mark White was the guy that everybody thought [if he won] could have beaten Clayton Williams. That is who the Republicans did not want, was Mark White. And she knew that. So she took him out. Smart move politically. It got her elected Governor. But she paid the price for it in the primary.*

Weeks thinks that, the terribly dangerous risk in the primary having paid off, the general election campaign offered her a much better opportunity to win:

> *Let me tell you, though, in many ways their whole strategy was that "if I can just get in the general*

*election, Clayton Williams will lose it. I'll just do
my deal, and he will just keep doing enough stupid
things that we will win." And they knew that and
they worked around that strategy. See, our [other
Republican statewide] candidates . . . stayed away
from Clayton. They didn't campaign with him, they
didn't appear with him. They didn't go any place
with him . . . And then all the mistakes Clayton
made. She did not make the same mistakes in the
general election that she did in the primary. She did
not come away as a cold-blooded executioner. She
didn't have to execute Clayton Williams. He did it
himself. She just made fun of him. She just said
"Can you believe this guy?" I mean, it wasn't cold-
blooded. (Interview, 14 October 1991)*

Our observations and our interviews with Richards campaign operatives incline us to the conclusion that the latter
would not at all disagree with Weeks' evaluation of campaign
strategy, and all but Karl Rove would agree on the role that
gender beliefs were playing in voters' assessments as they
rather wonderingly, disgustedly watched the show.

Scholarly research underscores Shipley's and Weeks' experience: without other bases for judgment, both men and
women will use candidates' sex as the basis for inferences
about not only candidates' gender-role traits but their general issue orientations. With little else to go on, voters will
assume that women candidates are better at the "compassion issues," more responsive, and more accountable, while
men are better at crisis management, toughness, and mili-
tary and foreign security issues. If, in an experimental setting, the candidates are endowed with instrumental or
socioemotional traits, they provoke even stronger gender-
typed inferences about candidates' leadership ability and issue expertise.

Women's leadership style, in these gender-typed inferences, most emphatically does not include being a "cold-
blooded executioner"; as Shipley said, Richards' negatives
reached such a high level that the campaign urgently sought
to establish her "hope, earth, faith, smile, mother quotient"

Claytie and the Lady

in an advertisement that was ostensibly about insurance reform. Some women leaders, such as former British Prime
Minister Margaret Thatcher, have been successful exceptions to the "mother quotient" expectation, but Thatcher
has also been called an "honorary man" and the "best man
in Parliament," as well as a "fishwife" (see Fraser 1990);
if she did not conform to many gender-role stereotypes, her
sex was nonetheless never ignored. Richards' sex, far from
being dismissable, became an enormously confounding
factor, as even Williams' "tough guy manhood" eventually
did, too.

On the question of issues, voters are reflecting reality:
historically (Tolleson Rinehart 1987; Sapiro 1986) and recently
(Stanley and Blair 1989; Thomas 1991), women have been
responsible for initiating policy that, without women's efforts, would be much less likely to find a place on the public
agenda, much less survive the policy process. There may be a
chicken-and-egg phenomenon here, since if health care,
children's well-being, education, and community concerns
are supposed to be appropriate concerns of women, women
leaders may believe that they *must* advocate such policies.
In other words, this is also a place where personality sub-
sumes issues, because of the recently diffused assumptions
that some sort of "feminine" political personality itself em-
bodies these issues.

Nonetheless—and keeping the chicken-and-egg dilemma
firmly in mind—women in office throughout the Western
democracies do, in the main, sponsor "compassion" policies
more frequently than do men (Haavio-Mannila et al. 1985).
A Republican woman who had served in the state legislature
in the 1970s drew on her own experience in concur-
ring with this common assessment of women's contribution to public policy. She does not share all or even most
of a Democratic woman's agenda. But she, too, told us that
some issues get attention, issues that men are not as likely
to address, because women office holders are there to give
voice to them. She also noted that there were transcending
issues, such as rape and child and spouse abuse, that cause
women to "band together" despite partisan or ideological
differences.

NEGATIVE CAMPAIGNING

The questions of leadership ability and style are much more difficult to analyze, partly because there have been few women in the most visible or powerful political offices, and partly because scholars have rarely turned their attention to the question of whether gender makes a difference to leadership. In the 1990 Texas gubernatorial election the question was further confounded by the campaign's rapid tendency to devolve on features of personality that may or may *not* have been evoking notions of leadership in voters' minds. Surely much in this heated campaign was stimulating affectual rather than cognitive reactions. Voters' wry disgust with the whole campaign is illustrated by a Dallas bumper sticker saying "I'd rather do drugs with Ann Richards than be serviced by Clayton Williams" (Ivins 1990).

While both male and female voters engage in gender-typed inferences about candidates, and while both sexes respond well to "androgynous" female candidates, androgyny poses a challenging balancing act for a woman in office (Pierce 1989): How does she appropriate the "masculine" characteristics valued in leaders without forfeiting the "feminine" qualities voters have also come to appreciate? And how will she be perceived? Social psychological research has documented that men and women respond quite differently even to the conversational style of women speakers. Female audiences prefer a woman to be direct, but male audiences see a direct woman as aggressive, and prefer her to be tentative—a quality *women* do not like to see in another woman (Carli 1990). Members of the audience may well not be conscious that they are relying on such gender-stereotyped cues; how can the woman addressing them, especially if the audience is composed of both men and women, avoid stimulating negative affect in either?

Drawing from other research, the perception of women office holders as particularly accountable and responsive may be a real advantage to women candidates, since people place great weight on their perceptions of procedural fairness when evaluating both policy outcomes and the legitimacy of leaders (Tyler, Rasinski, and McGraw 1985; Tyler 1986). Ann

Richards certainly had received high marks for accountability and responsiveness in her two terms as State Treasurer. But how highly do accountability and responsiveness, the traits for which voters are steadily rewarding women candidates, rank in judgments on women's suitability for the most powerful offices? Not only perceived characteristics but also the *priority* of those characteristics matter very much when individuals are judging others. Despite objective calculations showing that women make up about half of the worldwide contribution to subsistence, for example, the *perception* is that women's contribution is actually much less, or much less valued. Such perceptions have resulted in a symbolic division of labor, influencing the actual division, that values "men's work" as "important" and "women's work" as menial. In many cultures, women's only real bargaining power in personal relationships extends from their possession of tangible, recognized economic resources—that is, resources valued by men (Kidder, Fagan, and Cohn 1981).

The connection of these findings to the fortunes of women candidates, and especially to Ann Richards' electoral fortunes, is this: There is increasing documentation that women are now seen as acceptable, even desirable, in legislative office. More powerful offices, especially chief executive positions, are a different matter. Royal Masset, the research director of the Texas State Republican Party, is among others who assume that a woman candidate now has about a three-percent advantage over her male competitor in voter preference (interview, 13 May 1991). The Republican woman we spoke to also speculated that voters' acceptance of women has progressed from a "hill to climb twenty years ago" to "a significant disadvantage ten years ago" to a small advantage today. Research in political science suggests that, at least in legislative positions, male incumbency is the only remaining barrier to women candidates' success (Darcy, Welch, and Clark 1987).

But legislative offices (unless they are seats in the U.S. Senate) are simply not as highly valued as executive offices, and this creates the political "glass ceiling" for ambitious women. Executive leadership—as Governor, and certainly as President—is still correlated with instrumental, "masculine" characteristics. In the experimental work conducted by Huddy and Terkildsen (1993a), gender-typed candidates and issue orientations had their *poorest* fit with the "ideal" qualities of the presidency, and the trait-gender interaction was also *most* significant here. Of the eight women who ran as major party candidates for Governor in 1990, five—or over 60%— lost, in contrast to the 52% of men who ran for governor and lost. In 1992, all three women who ran as major party candidates for Governor—Democrats Deborah "Arnie" Arnesen of New Hampshire and Dorothy Bradley of Montana, and Republican Elizabeth Ann Leonard of Rhode Island—lost. Once again, gender cannot have been the only reason. The difficulty lies in establishing how much of a reason it was. Voters are now quite willing to vote for President a "qualified woman," in the language of the Gallup question asked since World War II, but gender stereotypes are still confounding judgments about what the "qualifications" should be. A man who planned to vote for Williams told reporter John Kelso (1990a) that he didn't have anything against a woman being governor but, he added, "Maybe a woman being president, that might be a little different." Elsewhere an East Texas man predicted a heavy turnout of Democratic men for Williams: "Men typically don't think women can do the job properly" (*Dallas Morning News*, 28 October 1990).

BREAKING THE COWBOY CODE

Richards entered the general election campaign with much less money and higher unfavorable voter opinions than did Clayton Williams. By the beginning of the summer of 1990, observers believed that Williams would have an easy victory, and by September, with a *Houston Chronicle* poll putting Williams ahead by 48% to 33%, observers were doubting that Richards could make up the lost ground. Richards' spirits were then further lowered, several people told us, by her fear that she would pull the whole Democratic ticket down. (Later, of course, as David Weeks said, it was the Republicans' turn to worry about their ticket floundering.) Williams presented himself as a "real man," as a large rancher and oilman, as someone who had made his own fortune and had created jobs.

He gloried in the myths of Texas' past, and wanted to make himself the evocative symbol of them. In many ways, these impulses are quite genuine. Molly Ivins puts it this way: "He really does wear cowboy boots and a cowboy hat all the time. He worships John Wayne, has a statue of Wayne in the lobby of his bank in Midland . . . he still gets tears in his eyes when-ever he hears the [Texas A&M University] fight song. He's got a trophy wife named Modesta. He hunts. He drinks. He occasionally gets into fistfights. And he believes the world simple" (1991: 278–279).

Richards was pejoratively depicted as a liberal—even a radical. Polls continued to find that Williams had a substan-tial lead among men and was running nearly even with Richards among women. An elderly couple in East Texas queried by a reporter provide colorful illustration of the state of things (Copelin 1990c):

> *"I just don't like seeing her whining and talking like a . . ." "A dying calf," interjects [Wilma Leavelle's] 83-year-old husband, A. Z. Leavelle, a retired school principal . . . The couple, married 58 years, fondly recall stories about Miriam "Ma" Ferguson, Texas' only woman governor . . . "Ma was OK because Pa was there to take care of things," A. Z. Leavelle explains.*

Williams began his string of remarkable gaffes in March, with the "rape joke," and he kept them coming. The polls did not show much disaffection with him early on, but the cumulative effect would be significant by the autumn. By October, an East Texas man could tell a reporter, "He's no cowboy. He's just a guy running around with a big hat de-grading women" (Hamilton 1990). While Richards and Mattox still "had each other by the throat," as Republican Milton Rister said, Williams had preceded the "rape joke" incident in mid-March by saying to the Washington Press Club, "I wouldn't be as comfortable in battling with a woman [Richards]. When I was at [Texas] A&M [University] it was an all-male, all-military school; two years in the Army; build-ing [oil] pipelines, it was a male workforce in the field . . . I've never been in an adversarial position with a woman except once way back when I had a divorce, and I lost." Richards responded, "I don't want to be his mother. I want to be Governor of Texas" (Attlesey, 1990).

In April, Williams admitted to an inquisitive journalist that he had paid prostitutes, presumably in brothels near the Mexican border, as a youth (he did not admit any more recent engagements). "It's part of the fun of growing up in West Texas," he said. "The houses were the only place you got serviced then . . ." (Means 1990; Gravois 1990b). Journalist Molly Ivins (1991) and Republican consultant Karl Rove believe that the Richards campaign had talked sufficiently long and hard, if informally, about Williams' proclivities that the curiosity of the enterprising press was finally piqued. In other words, especially in Rove's view, Williams was set up by the Richards campaign. The Richards campaign operatives do maintain that their conscious strategy was one of forcing the mistakes that Williams made (see the Rogers and Shipley interviews), although whether this particular incident was the product of that strategy is not something we can ascertain. Set up or not, whether Williams was demonstrating appropriate leadership traits when he admitted to frequenting brothels is another question entirely.

Admitting that he had gone to prostitutes might have been acceptable, but Williams angered many in the Hispanic community with his evocation of Anglo boys in Mexican bordellos, and his use of the verb "serviced" offended many women (Means 1990). In mid-July, he was to make the situation worse by trying to explain that tricky verb "serviced" to a *U.S. News and World Report* reporter, and saying that, on the ranch, bulls serviced cows, and that he was just trying to find a "nice, polite term for f——" (Copelin 1990a). Also in July, the Williams campaign erroneously claimed that Richards had received contributions from Jane Fonda, said that Fonda was a "traitor," and insinuated that Richards was as well (Attlesey 1990a); he further called Richards an "honorary lesbian" because of gay groups' support of her (*Texas Observer* 1990). His difficulty in seeing women in other than sexual terms was becoming hard not to notice.

Through the summer, respected journals such as *Texas Monthly* and the liberal but investigative *Texas Observer* began questioning Williams' business dealings; the results of their investigations began to appear in the autumn. Among the most controversial was the revelation that, in water-starved West Texas, he had pumped Comanche Springs dry to irrigate his own land, thereby parching all the land to the east of his own (Kelso 1990b). At the same time, though, the press—and voters—wondered when Ann Richards was going to "do something": when would she present a clear image and program? She had talked about the "New Texas," but what did that mean? (Democratic media consultant Mark McKinnon had told us that it "means just that. Not the Old Texas"—but he said he worried continually that the debate over the meaning of the phrase would never end; interview, 14 May 1991.) The candidate herself was aware of the strains in her campaign: "Everyone wanted to let Ann be Ann," she told *Texas Monthly*, "And they all had different Anns" (Swartz 1990: 120). She had been constantly on the defensive, respond-ing to Williams' attacks—but without the money to respond in television ads until very late in the summer—and unable to play to her strengths (Attlesey 1990b).

In mid-September, the momentum in the campaign be-gan to change. The Richards campaign emphasized the issue of insurance reform, a sore spot in Texas, as Williams' ClayDesta National Bank began to come under investigation for automobile insurance irregularities (Kuempel and Slater 1990). In August, the Richards campaign had inaugurated a series of television commercials, "Meet Clayton Williams," stressing the offensive remarks and questions about his busi-ness practices (Copelin 1990b). Milton Rister, Williams' as-sociate in ClayDesta Communications and in the campaign, told us that, ironically, the February plane crash that killed Williams' closest business partners "probably cost him the election" because those same associates would have been there in the autumn to perform damage control on allega-tions against Williams' business practices (interview, 3 Au-gust 1993). If Republican Karl Rove is right—and we think he is—that the "numbers didn't move" after Williams' earli-est gaffes, then the Richards campaign deserves a great deal of credit for "moving the numbers" in the fall, by pounding home the accumulation of Williams malapropisms, and successfully keeping them at the forefront of voters' "running tally" images of him (see Lodge, McGraw, and Stroh 1989, on candidate image formation). And the Williams campaign appeared unable to control its candidate or mitigate the damage being done. At the same time, though, that Richards was able to be more successful and vigorous, taking the offensive against Williams, she had only just begun to succeed in presenting a positive image of herself.

As observers believed that Richards' ads were beginning to have a positive effect, Clayton Williams lent her a hand (though not a handshake). In the course of defending himself and ClayDesta National, his bank, against charges of wrongdoing, he said of his opponent that he would "head and hoof her and drag her through the dirt" (Slater and Garcia 1990). This, for non-Texans, is the process of throwing a calf down and tying its head and hooves together in a way that immobilizes it. But what with bulls servicing cows in July, and heading and hoofing in September, observers were beginning to note Williams' penchant for likening women to cattle. In late September, Williams, confident that his lead was insuperable, offended sensibilities once again by responding to Richards' claim that she was closing the gap between them with, "I hope she didn't go back to drinking again" (Copelin 1990d). Rister told us that the campaign learned only *after* he made the comment that they were already dropping in the polls. He argues that "the thing that hurt us most was that the President signed the [1990] tax bill. We dropped from a twelve-point to a six-point lead in the next poll . . . when Claytie said [that] he didn't know . . ." (interview, 3 August 1993). The color and drama of the campaign showed no signs of giving way to a substantive policy debate, and the color that Claytie was contributing was not helping his cause.

In October, Claytie broke the cowboy code for the last time. In Dallas, attempting to recreate an event in John Tower's 1978 senate race, he got the attention of a television crew, confronted Richards, called her a "liar," and made a great point of refusing to shake hands with her (Germond and Witcover 1990; Ward 1990; McNeely 1990a; Jamieson 1992). That did it, in the minds of many. The pointed face-to-face discourtesy to a woman deeply offended many of his traditional supporters, who might have allowed many of his earlier salty comments. Both of us frequently heard this comment on his behavior: "He may talk like a cowboy, and dress like a cowboy, but he ain't no cowboy"—because a cowboy would never refuse to shake a lady's hand. For some men and for more women, he was becoming "just a guy in a big hat degrading women." Richards' own Achilles' heel, the question of whether she had ever used drugs other than alcohol, also resurfaced at this time. A former Mattox aide went to Republican campaign officials with the charge that he had seen her using cocaine at a party following a fundraising event in 1977. Witnesses came forward to say that she had not been at the party, and no other evidence was forthcoming. The charge went no further (Copelin 1990e)—apart from looking like Mattox and Williams "degrading a woman" again—perhaps because Williams was about to displace its effect by precipitating yet more criticism of himself.

At the end of October, the rape gaffe resurfaced in a way most haunting to many women: A rapist, in the course of his assault, had quoted Williams. On the day the rapist was sentenced, less than a week before the election, the victim said, "Speaking from personal experience, rape is anything but a joke, and at no point, Mr. Williams, was I able to relax and enjoy it" (Rothschild 1990). In this same dreadful last week for the Williams organization, the final two Williams imbroglios occurred. First, Williams said in an interview on a Dallas television station that he could recall neither the sole constitutional amendment on the ballot nor the way he had voted on it. The amendment, in fact, would have weakened gubernatorial appointment powers—among the Texas Governor's most significant powers. Lapsing in his tough masculinity, he explained that his wife Modesta "told me what to do" when the couple had voted by absentee ballot two weeks before (Slater and Attlesey 1990)—another couple composed, as the saying goes, of a strong woman pretending to be weak and a weak man pretending to be strong? Milton Rister told us that this and similar events were the result of a serious mistake on the campaign's part—that of "the decision to avoid Ann Richards. There was a fear that Ann Richards would do better in debate because she's wittier, more seasoned—all of that's true. But if you *have* to do it, do it early. But a decision was made to avoid her. Then Claytie was in the position of debating the *press* instead of Ann Richards, and [when that is the case] the press controls the format" (interview, 3 August 1993). This is certainly the context in which the embarrassing revelation arose that Williams didn't know what was on the ballot or how he had voted on it.

Only days later, after repeated evasion when asked why he would not release his income tax returns as Richards had done every year since 1982, the news that the multimillionaire had paid no taxes in 1986 washed over the campaign (Attlesey and Slater 1990; Attlesey 1990c; Slater 1990b).

Suddenly, it was a race. Richards, after trailing from the beginning, had pulled nearly even among those who had decided for whom they would vote. Richards' negatives were still high, but Williams' harsh campaigning and behavior had caused his own negatives to climb, and the once high-flying candidate ran television ads apologizing for his mistakes and asking for voters' support (Kuempel 1990). But in late October, the Richards campaign began reminding voters of every controversial Williams statement, ending with a voice asking incredulously, "Governor Williams?"

THE UNDECIDED VOTER

On election day, the voters decided "perhaps not." Miraculous as it seemed to Richards' supporters, women had turned overwhelmingly to her, while Williams' support among men had slipped and his support among women had seriously eroded, as Table 4.2 and Figure 4.1 make clear. More women had voted for Richards than men had voted for Williams, and Williams fell well below his campaign's target for Hispanic voters (McNeely 1990b). Even silk-stocking Republican Dallas County went narrowly for Richards (Flick 1990).

There is almost universal agreement that if Williams had been a more modern figure, he could have won. Molly Ivins said, and most people would concur, that he embarrassed urban Texans with his crudeness and gaucherie, while

TABLE 4.2. Support for Richards and Williams in the Final Month of the Campaign, by Sex

Leaning toward:	6 Oct.* M %	6 Oct.* W %	18 Oct.* M %	18 Oct.* W %	23 Oct.* M %	23 Oct.* W %	29 Oct.* M %	29 Oct.* W %	2 Nov.* M %	2 Nov.* W %	6 Nov.* M %	6 Nov.* W %
Richards	27.3	44.5	36.7	47.9	33.0	49.5	34.0	46.2	32.8	47.3	44.0	59.0
Williams	60.5	42.9	52.8	39.2	53.2	35.9	52.5	40.1	52.1	38.0	56.0	41.0
Undecided	12.2	12.6	10.5	12.9	13.8	14.6	14.5	13.7	15.0	14.7	—	—

Source: Data for 6 October through 2 November supplied by Shipley and Associates; data for 6 November (election day) supplied by Voter Research and Surveys. Marginal frequencies supplied by both sources were analyzed by authors using SAS-PC. In legend, M = men; W = women. Prior to election day, percentages for Richards and Williams supporters include those who had already made up their minds and those "leaning toward" one candidate or the other. The percentages on election day are for all Richards and Williams voters; those voting for the Libertarian candidate are not included.

*Differences are significant at *p* < .01

The Unfolding of a Gubernatorial Campaign

FIGURE 4.1. Progress of Gender Gap, the Final Month of the Campaign

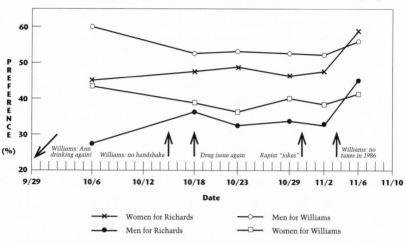

Source: See text.

Richards very consciously tried to appear strong enough to be Governor—so strong, in fact, that her humor, one of her most appealing qualities, was all but sacrificed. The "ranch foreman" image of leadership is gone now; it was unavailable to Williams, although he did not know it. Richards, on the other hand, managed to project "frontierswoman" qualities of strength and a populism that, in their way, also drew on Texas myths, while appearing very modern indeed. Richards said she had told her children, "You're not going to recognize your mother by the time they get through with me" (Slater 1990a). In the end, Richards was tough enough.

Many voters, though, *were* genuinely undecided until the last moment: this was not an easy race to judge. Richards' momentum grew with women, and Williams lost momentum with many groups. We have constructed theoretical perspectives and drawn on the perspectives of political elites and journalists. From these we have derived a number of insights about the election. Now we shall turn to the voters, to see what more we can learn.

I think it will be very interesting if we get more cases like Ann Richards, a woman who raised her children and had a twenty-three-year marriage before she went into politics . . . I think Ann Richards has shown that it's not too late.

—MOLLY IVINS, interview with the authors, 14 May 1991

CHAPTER 5

Gender Roles and Gender Politics

Ann Richards' political career is an extraordinary phenomenon. And in the course of pursuing that career, she has come to bear the heavy weight of expectations resting on the shoulders of all of the women in the very select group of high office holders that she joined in 1990. Because of her forceful personality, and because of the fables and myths attached to the very large state she was elected to govern, she is a far more vivid role model than most—other women governors (with the possible exception of "Ma" herself!) have not attracted the attention or notoriety that Richards has. But the qualities that, to many, make her a role model, or at least a subject for admiring observation, make her a threat to others, and a puzzle to still others. She is seen as "everywoman," but of course she is also unique. Her election was a "breakthrough" of the political glass ceiling, but could any other woman have duplicated it?

It is our task now to see if we can discern some of these intricate patterns of response and judgment among the voters in whose hands her fate finally rested. We do this with statistical analysis. For those who are unfamiliar with the techniques we use, we have tried to provide straightforward explanations of what we have done in the pages to follow and in the notes section. We also provide a nonstatistical "portrait" of the voters, based on our findings, at the end of the chapter.

INTER- AND INTRASEX DIFFERENCES
IN THE VOTE CHOICE

On election day, in most cases, men and women were a mirror image of each other.[1] Women with less education voted in very large numbers for Richards, while the most educated women were deeply divided between Richards and Williams. Men with the most education, in contrast, overwhelmingly voted for Williams, while his majority among less educated men was a slim one. In both cases, higher education may be a surrogate for professional employment: men in the professional and managerial classes may have voted for Williams despite the gaffes because of the expectation that a Republican would benefit business interests, and that Richards would be too "liberal," despite her good working relationship with business while she was Treasurer. Women, on the other hand, may have given gender issues, and most notably Williams' apparent attitudes about women, the higher priority, as evidence from the American National Election Studies, presented later on, seems to confirm. Richards received the vote of an enormous number of Black and Hispanic women, and minority men also turned out very strongly for her. White women, in contrast, were narrowly split between Richards and Williams, while white men gave Claytie the lion's share of their vote. The gender gap was present in every age cohort, but it was most noticeable among the youngest voters.

Voters strove for consistency between their ideological self-identification, their partisanship, and their choice for Governor, as Table 5.1 makes evident. But once again, gender gaps are markedly evident: more conservative and Republican women gave their votes to Ann Richards than did their male counterparts, and more liberal and Democratic men voted for Williams than did similarly identified women. The gender gap was very strong among Independents: nearly 60% of women without a party identification voted for Richards, and a similar proportion of Independent men chose Williams. Abortion, an issue that in many ways reflects not only moral and ideological questions but the difference between Old and New Texas, was the one area where men and women did not seem quite so different, although it could not

TABLE 5.1. Intra- and Intersex Percentage Differences among Exit-Poll Respondents, by Vote Choice

	Men		Women	
	Richards	Williams	Richards	Williams
A. Education	*		*	
Less than high school	48.4	51.6	60.9	39.1
Some college	47.0	53.0	55.1	44.9
College or more	27.6	72.4	49.7	50.3
B. Race	*		*	
White	36.7	63.3	48.9	51.1
Black	84.4	15.6	93.0	7.0
Hispanic	61.9	38.1	78.4	21.6
C. Age	†		†	
18–29	37.5	62.5	53.7	46.3
30–44	43.0	57.0	59.9	40.1
45–59	47.1	52.9	64.6	35.4
60 and older	49.5	50.5	58.8	41.2
D. Ideology	*		*	
Liberal	63.3	36.7	87.0	13.0
Moderate	59.7	40.3	68.7	31.3
Conservative	25.1	74.9	36.0	64.0
E. Party identification	*		*	
Democrat	81.4	18.6	89.2	10.8
Independent	40.3	59.7	58.5	41.5
Republican	14.1	85.9	24.0	76.0
F. Abortion	*		*	
Always legal	58.5	41.5	71.6	28.4
In some circumstances	40.0	60.0	57.7	42.3
Never legal	31.5	68.5	38.0	62.0
G. Most negative campaign?	*		*	
Richards	16.0	84.0	22.8	77.2
Williams	87.0	13.0	93.7	6.3
Both	45.2	54.8	51.6	48.4
H. When vote decided	*		*	
In the last week	52.9	47.1	64.3	35.7
In the last month	55.9	44.1	79.8	20.2
Before that	41.7	58.3	57.1	42.9
I. Sex of candidate	‡		‡	
Most important factor	35.3	64.7	73.1	26.9
One of several	43.1	56.9	71.6	28.4
Not important	48.9	51.1	59.1	40.9

Source: Voter Research and Surveys, General Election Exit Poll: State Files, 1990 (ICPSR Study No. 9604).

*Differences significant at $p < .01$ by vote choice within each sex.

†Differences significant at $p < .05$ by vote choice within each sex.

‡No significant difference by vote choice within each sex.

erase the gender gap. A majority of pro-choice men, and larger numbers of pro-choice women, chose Richards. On the pro-life side, Williams certainly appeared to be in favor of banning abortion except to save a woman's life, even though the strength and consistency of his position was apparently not enough to satisfy the leaders of anti-abortion groups (Copelin 1990; Gravois 1990a). He nonetheless won majorities of both pro-life men and pro-life women. The determined pro-choice voter would certainly prefer Richards, and the equally determined pro-life voter had no place to turn but Williams. But among voters who believed abortion should be legal in only some circumstances, there was a reversion to the typical gendered pattern, with women more likely to vote for Richards, and men more likely to vote for Williams.

Who had the most negative campaign? Less than a half of one percent of voters who completed the questionnaire thought that neither campaign had been negative, for the very good reason that both campaigns were. Among those who felt Richards had been the more negative, both men and women gave their votes to Williams. Those who thought Williams had hit the lowest blows voted for Richards. But among those who thought both had been equally negative, gender was decisive, with a majority of women choosing Ann and a majority of men opting for Claytie. Expert observers thought, by the autumn, that the campaign was alienating voters, and as we recall, there were unusually large numbers of people who claimed that they had not yet decided how to vote in late October. In the exit poll, almost 20% of respondents refused to answer the question as to when they had made their decision, but of those who did, those who decided latest were more likely to have decided in favor of Richards than Williams, supporting universal assumptions that the pileup of gaffes finally damaged his candidacy beyond repair. Although no causal relationship can be asserted, recall that Figure 4.1 in Chapter 4 also suggests an association between media coverage of the campaign's final controversies and shifts in voter preferences. Men who had decided more than a month before the election were more likely to choose Williams and gave him a majority; likewise, Richards had a firm core of women supporters long before the election. Too much can be made of this question, since people may have sincere difficulty in knowing when they arrived at a decision. But the results here do suggest that Ann had motivated an intensely loyal core of supporters who were not going to be shaken by a bitter campaign. Claytie, in contrast, was virtually unknown before the Republican primary, his support was not of long standing, and his appeal seemed finally to wear thin.

The questionnaire asked voters whether the sex of the candidate was the single most important factor, one of several important factors, or not an important factor in the voter's decision. Only approximately 21% of men and women admitted that it was even one among several important factors, as we discussed at greater length in Chapter 3. Of those groups, over 70% of women voted for Richards, and a majority, though not a significant majority, of men voted for Williams. The gender gap among men and women who said that the sex of the candidate was *not* important was smaller but still evident. The fact that most voters said sex was not important, even though the gender gap in this race was a yawning chasm and the prisms of gender were always present to refract candidate images, is difficult to interpret with any empirical security. But our analysis, joined to extant research, suggests four possibilities. The finding may mean that, even in an anonymous survey, people wished to give the socially desirable response: voting for a candidate just because that candidate shares one's sex is contrary to civic education. It could indicate that many voters were not consciously using gender as an organizing principle in their decision making, even while it nonetheless persisted as a subtext. It may indicate a substantive gap in issue preferences and political outlook—that men share one orientation, and women share another, and the candidates each represented the male or female "worldview"; there is literature to support such a gender gap in policy preferences, but the literature of American political behavior is cautionary when it comes to assuming that voters' issue and candidate preferences are so flawlessly knit together. The fourth possibility concerns the additionally confounding factor of the *treatment* of gender in the campaign: few male candidates in the last two decades were as controversially "male" or offensive to, and about, women as Clayton Williams was. Even if one did not personally care a great deal about his remarks, the media attention they attracted made them hard to ignore. The findings as well as the campaign reportage hint that all four explanations may have merit. Recall that Dianne Feinstein received different reactions as a California *gubernatorial* candidate in 1990 than she did as a *Senate* candidate in 1992—and that she lost the gubernatorial race, while emerging almost easily triumphant from her Senate campaign. Ann Richards, too, had sailed to easy and convincing victories in her two State Treasurer races. Why, then, was her gubernatorial campaign such a bloody struggle? We believe that her sex, varying gender-role beliefs on the part of voters, and gendered perceptions of leadership all played roles too important to ignore, even if they are too intricate to be understood easily.

The gender gaps remain ever present, but voters' choices of the "two or three issues mattering most" show a campaign not only of gender but of New versus Old Texas. The four issues most often mentioned by voters in the exit poll were education, ethics, crime, and the state economy. Education and ethics concerns drove voters to Richards, and those men and women who were most activated by fear of crime chose Williams. But of those who were most motivated by concern about the state economy, the men were more likely to vote for Williams, while the women chose Richards—this, no doubt, is the Old Texas of ranching and oil versus the New Texas service economy.

Journalist Molly Ivins, without reference to the exit-poll data, said that as she was covering the campaign, she heard from many women for whom Richards' success seemed like an invalidation of their own traditional lives (interview, 14 May 1991). For women who saw Richards not as a threat but as a role model, in contrast, it was Williams who was "extreme" and "negative."

Ann Richards enjoyed the ardent support of a significant number of women from the moment she entered the race.

But for many women, the campaign was a difficult one, pulling them in opposite directions. For women who might have experienced cognitive dissonance—because they were pro-choice on abortion but "fiscally conservative" Republicans, or because their socialization and culture all prompted them toward traditional roles for women, with Richards representing modern roles, yet Williams offending against traditional morality—dissonance was apparently resolved at last in a vote for Richards. If beliefs about abortion are also surrogates for traditional moral beliefs, that may even help explain why women more opposed to abortion took longer to decide to vote for Ann Richards. Despite Richards' vehement pro-choice stance, Williams' morality may finally have been judged to be too dubious to merit support—and, indeed, his anti-abortion position was never delivered forcefully enough to satisfy pro-life elites. His anti-abortion stance never came across as part of a clearly articulated social conservative philosophy, perhaps not surprisingly in a man who did not appear to have thought much about political questions until he ran for Governor. If anything, the abortion issue worked against him when journalists asked, with heavy irony, whether he had thought about contraception and abortion when he had been patronizing the brothels across the Mexican border.

WHAT TEXANS THINK ABOUT POLITICS

In the 1990 Texas gubernatorial race, the bitter controversy of the campaign may have driven potential voters away, but the analysis below suggests that nonvoters did not require this race to remove themselves from the political arena as active participants. Of the 144 respondents to the 1990 American National Election Study, 83 people (58.9%) said they did not vote in the election, 18 (12.8%) claimed to have voted for Clayton Williams, and 40 (28.4%) claimed to have voted for Ann Richards; 3 individuals' voting behavior could not be ascertained. Although we cannot verify respondents' actual voting behavior, we believe that the proportion who claimed to have voted, especially for Richards, is slightly inflated. Both this and the tiny numbers involved invite extreme caution while interpreting the results of our analysis. What we remain interested in, however, is the correspondence of respondents' attitudes and participatory behavior to their reports of what they did on election day.

Tables 5.2 and 5.3 show survey respondents' levels of attentiveness to politics, participation, system evaluations and internal efficacy, and knowledge about political figures and the party composition of the U.S. House and Senate. These levels demonstrate the internal psychological resources and behavior of Williams voters, of nonvoters, and of Richards voters, as well those of all men and all women. Respondents' reports of their own degree of liberalism or conservatism, their views on appropriate levels of federal spending in a variety of different policy domains, their assessments of the degree of sex discrimination women face on the job, and their "feeling-thermometer"[2] ratings of both candidates and numerous groups in society are analyzed with a view to establishing the degree of ideological consistency (or the lack thereof) and the policy preferences among the three groups as well as between each sex. Finally, after constructing multidimensional scales measuring several dimensions of psychological resources and policy preference (see Appendix B for scale construction and frequencies), we employ the scales, ideological self-placement, the candidate and women's movement feeling thermometers, and the assessment of sex discrimination in discriminant analyses that permit us to distinguish Williams voters from nonvoters from Richards voters.

All the analyses point to a characterization of Texans that resonates well with most current perspectives on American political behavior generally, with the politics of gender roles, and with the events of the gubernatorial campaign. Nonvoters could be called "the remote ones"—they are not noticeably alienated or angry, and their ideology and policy preferences are quite moderate. They are simply disengaged from and disinterested in politics. Williams voters, on the other hand, are the "engaged and angry." They are interested in politics and relatively active; and they are fairly internally efficacious (they have confidence in themselves as capable of

TABLE 5.2 Psychological Resources, by Voter Status and Sex

	Williams %	Nonvoters %	Richards %	Men %	Women %
A. Knowledge (mean)[b]	3.8	1.8	3.6	3.3	1.9
B. Attentiveness					
a. Interested[a]	100.0	53.0	90.0	77.8	62.5
b. Read newspaper[a]	88.9	41.0	85.0	68.1	52.8
c. Watched TV[c]	88.3	60.2	75.0	79.2	56.9
d. Discuss politics[b]	72.2	64.6	82.5	80.6	62.0
C. Participation					
a. Voted 1988[a]	100.0	31.3	97.4	62.9	56.5
b. Influenced[a/.02]	27.8	10.8	40.0	30.6	13.9
c. Button/sticker	16.7	7.2	15.0	6.9	13.9
d. Attended meeting	5.6	4.8	15.0	11.1	4.2
e. Work party/candidate	11.1	1.2	7.5	2.8	5.6
f. Gave money[a]	16.7	1.2	0.0	5.6	1.4
D. System evaluations					
a. Trust govt.	33.4	31.6	48.6	33.8	40.3
b. Doesn't waste money	16.7	38.5	46.1	31.8	43.4
c. Benefits all	22.2	34.7	30.6	29.9	32.3
d. Not many crooks	38.9	48.6	58.3	40.7	50.0
E. Internal efficacy					
a. Pub ofcls care[a]	33.3	13.8	25.6	22.8	17.1
b. Have say	50.0	29.5	33.4	31.4	35.3
c. Pol not compl[/.02]	22.3	19.0	28.9	31.5	11.8

Source: 1990 American National Election Study data; consult Appendix B for coding information.

[a]Differences significant at $p < .01$ by voting groups only.
[b]Differences significant at $p < .01$ by voting groups and by sex.
[c]Differences significant at $p < .01$ by sex only.

For differences by sex of $.10 > p > .01$, significance is given to right of slash. No superscript means no significant difference. For mean scores, difference is from analysis of variance.

Claytie and the Lady

TABLE 5.3. Ideology and Beliefs about Federal Spending, by Voter Status and Sex

	Williams %	Nonvoters %	Richards %	Men %	Women %
I. Self-placement[.03/]					
a. Liberal	5.9	32.7	37.9	30.4	28.9
b. Moderate	29.4	34.6	41.4	37.5	33.3
c. Conservative	64.7	32.7	20.7	32.1	37.8
II. *Increase* federal spending for:					
a. Environment[.07/]	33.3	46.3	66.7	54.9	43.9
b. Foreign aid	0.0	5.0	2.7	4.2	3.0
c. Fighting AIDS[.03/]	38.9	72.0	69.4	67.6	67.6
d. Social security	38.9	66.7	55.3	56.3	65.2
e. War on drugs[.03/]	55.6	66.3	74.4	63.9	70.4
f. Food stamps[a]	5.6	16.7	17.9	9.9	20.9
g. Public schools	58.8	59.3	65.8	64.3	58.0
h. Help homeless[.02/]	33.3	67.1	78.9	69.0	64.3
i. Child care[a]	22.2	54.9	64.1	54.2	54.3
j. Assist Blacks[a]	5.9	40.7	37.8	36.6	34.3
k. Space program	16.7	18.3	5.4	18.1	11.8
III. Sex discrimination on job					
a. A lot	27.8	22.8	33.3	29.0	25.7
b. Some	66.7	68.4	56.4	60.9	65.7
c. None	5.6	8.9	10.3	10.1	8.6

Source: 1990 American National Election Study data; consult Appendix B for coding information.

[a]Differences significant at $p < .01$ by voting groups only.

For differences by voter status of $.10 > p > .01$, significance is given to left of slash. No superscript means no significant difference. For mean scores, difference is from analysis of variance.

carrying out competent citizen roles). But their assessment of the system in which they participate is quite harsh, they are conservative, and they heartily dislike current government spending priorities.

Richards voters, in contrast to the other two groups, are the "modest hopefuls." They eagerly consume political information; they are gregarious—they try to influence others, and attend political meetings more than do the other groups. While even a majority of nonvoters say they discuss politics with family and friends, only a fifth of them do so at least three times a week, whereas 38.5% of Williams voters have political conversations that often. But almost half of Richards voters (48.5%) find themselves talking about politics at least three times a week (figures not shown). The "modest hopefuls" are more generous in their assessment of the system, and more supportive of government spending to help others. They are modest because they lack the internal efficacy that might be expected to accompany their relatively higher rates of attentiveness and activity. They seem to be optimistic about the system and its ability to solve problems, even though they do not believe they themselves are especially important actors in it.

To those who desire an informed citizenry, the levels of knowledge of political leaders and the political system shown in Table 5.2 are a matter for concern. Very, very few Texans can correctly recognize seven national and international political figures or say which party holds a majority of seats in each House of Congress (see Appendix B). On average, both Williams and Richards voters are twice as knowledgeable as are nonvoters, the latter once again manifesting their disinterest in politics. But even the more avid Williams and Richards voters, on average, can get less than half the items on a simple practical knowledge test right. To those who long for women's complete political development, the difference in political knowledge between men and women is equally depressing.

With regard to other gender differences, Texas is a somewhat exaggerated picture of America. There are few significant differences between men's and women's attentiveness or participation, but those few are instructive. Men continue to discuss politics and to try to persuade others more often than do women. Women are slightly less likely to follow politics in the newspapers or on television, and slightly more likely to believe that politics is too complicated for them to understand, than is true of men. These particular findings suggest the lingering power of traditional gender-role admonitions that politics is not women's business—perhaps Ann

Richards will make a difference in this regard since, as journalist Molly Ivins told us, "Every schoolgirl in Texas can
dream now" (interview, 14 May 1991). Since education is
one of the most important resources in women's political
development (Duverger 1955; Sapiro 1983), cohort replacement (the replacement of one age group, as it ages and dies,
with the next youngest age group) may also effect change.
In this sample, men have significantly more education than
do women, but generational trends are closing the overall gap since younger women are, on the whole, better educated than their older female counterparts and are even
slowly becoming better educated than men of their same
age group.

As Table 5.4 shows, we see that feeling-thermometer ratings of groups in society comport reasonably well with the
general characterization of nonvoters as "the remote ones,"
Williams voters as the "engaged and angry," and of "modest
hopefuls" in the Richards camp. Even Williams voters, by
the end, were cool enough toward him that they do not significantly differ from other groups. All three groups also felt
similar sympathy for Black people and the poor, as we see
from the scores of considerable average warmth that they
elicit. Weak but still significant differences delineated reactions to "abortion supporters" and "abortion opponents,"
with the former group faring least well (perhaps the term "pro-
choice groups" would have elicited more sympathy than "supporters of abortion," particularly among women). Conservatives, labor unions, the women's movement, welfare recipi-
ents, environmentalists, liberals, and Ann Richards herself
all elicited sharp distinctions among voting groups, while Ann
Richards was the only target of notably different affect on
the basis of sex: women's lower rating of her, although very
substantially higher than their rating of Clayton Williams,
is, we believe, the manifestation of poignant ambivalence in
gender-role ideologies. The other groups represent more or-
thodox political targets, with Williams voters giving the
lowest ratings to all but conservatives, Richards voters giving the highest ratings, even to conservatives, and "the remote ones" falling in between, but lying closer to Richards'

TABLE 5.4. Feeling Thermometers and Scales, by Voter Status and Sex

	Williams	Nonvoter	Richards	Men	Women
I. Feeling Thermometers					
a. Ann Richards[b]	34.4	65.5	76.2	68.0	60.3
b. Clayton Williams	48.9	42.0	33.1	39.9	40.8
c. Pro-abort.[.07/.02]	45.3	35.4	51.1	48.0	34.9
d. Blacks	71.9	73.6	77.2	73.7	74.6
e. Conservatives[a]	76.4	58.6	65.8	63.6	63.0
f. Labor unions[a]	39.7	60.7	66.5	58.1	61.1
g. Women's movement[a]	45.8	72.7	78.9	70.7	71.6
h. Those on welfare[a]	35.8	57.1	59.6	51.9	58.6
i. Environmentalists[a]	64.4	83.0	83.3	79.7	81.2
j. Liberals[a]	36.4	54.6	64.4	56.7	52.2
k. Poor people	74.4	83.7	79.1	80.3	82.2
l. Anti-abortion[.03/]	61.9	64.6	47.8	53.9	65.0
II. Summary Scales					
a. Attentiveness[b]	3.44	2.19	3.33	3.06	2.35
b. Participation[a]	1.82	0.54	1.77	1.19	0.96
c. System evaluations	1.11	1.53	1.81	1.27	1.38
d. Internal efficacy	-0.55	-1.23	-0.71	-0.77	-1.21
e. Federal spending[a]	0.06	3.54	4.33	3.27	3.42

Source: 1990 American National Election Study data; consult Appendix B for coding information.

[a]Differences significant at $p < .01$ by voter status only.

[b]Differences significant at $p < .01$ by voter status and by sex.

For differences of $.10 > p > .01$, significance is given to left (by voter status) or right (by sex) of slash. No superscript means no significant difference. For mean scores, difference is from analysis of variance.

"modest hopefuls" than to Williams' "angry and engaged" supporters.

Table 5.4 also shows the mean rankings of the multidimensional scales constructed from attentiveness, participation, efficacy, and federal spending questions. These will also join the knowledge scale in the discriminant analyses presented in Tables 5.7 and 5.8. But Table 5.4 forces us to note with a by-now-familiar dismay that, as the United States as a whole, few people in Texas are knowledgeable or participatory, that most people feel inefficacious, lacking confidence in their abilities as political actors, and that Williams voters—the "engaged and angry"—care for few federal spending programs and have a positive esthesia for disliking and mistrusting government. So far, our very small number of voters and nonvoters from the 1990 American National Election Study seems to confirm exactly the impressions we had drawn in Chapters 3 and 4.

GENDER CONSCIOUSNESS, GENDER SYMPATHY, AND FEMINISM

The Board of Overseers of the American National Election Studies seized an opportunity with the 1991 pilot study: it was designed not only to test new indicators in preparation for the 1992 survey, but to be a panel study of attitudes toward the Persian Gulf War,[3] meaning that over 65% of respondents to the 1990 American National Election Study were reinterviewed in 1991. This, in turn, offers us an opportunity, since another principal goal of the pilot study was to test new measures of gender consciousness, feminism, and beliefs about men's and women's roles in the domains of government and politics, business and industry, and the family.

We cannot make as much of this opportunity as we would like, unfortunately, because the new gender measures were asked of only approximately one-third of the 1991 sample.[4] In the case of Texas, this means that our "sample" is reduced from 144 respondents to the 1990 study to 35 respondents who were reinterviewed *and* asked the gender questions. Thus, readers are warned that the findings to follow must be viewed with caution and must not be taken as representative of all Texans, since small sample size and very large margin of error attaches great risk to any attempt at extrapolation.

The respondents, however, *can* be considered at the very least to represent themselves. Since we know their voting behavior and other measures of their orientations toward politics in 1990, as well as their "feeling-thermometer" reactions to Ann Richards and Clayton Williams, the desire to examine the relationship between these things and their reactions to some of the new gender questions is well-nigh irresistible. We have not resisted, and the relationships are presented below. We must emphasize that the results must be treated with caution, and we are prevented by small sample size from subdividing the respondents in too many ways. Thus, we cannot make sharp distinctions between what might be *gender consciousness* in women respondents and *feminist sympathy* among men, because we cannot imperil this analysis of small numbers of people further by subdividing them into the two sexes. Readers are also warned that considerations of statistical significance have less meaning here, since we cannot purport to treat such a small sample as representative of all Texans. Nonetheless, what emerges from the findings is telling.

Of the several new questions about feminism and women's roles, five seemed particularly evocative of the feelings that might be stirred by gender and politics in 1990 and 1991. Whether respondents pay attention to news stories about women, whether they are ever angered about women's treatment in society, whether they think of themselves as feminist, and what their judgment is on how women can best improve their position (by independent action or by working together)—all, on the surface, tap awareness of gender differences and, perhaps to a lesser degree, the politicization of that awareness. The last item, presented only to women respondents, was intended to tap women's group identification (see Conover and Sapiro 1992, for discussion of all the new measures; see also Conover 1988a, 1988b; Sigel and Welchel 1986; Sapiro 1990; Tolleson Rinehart 1992, for discussions of group sympathy and gender consciousness). We see in Table 5.5 that, even given the enormous margins of error that must apply, Richards voters are far more sensitive to gender, more likely to think of themselves as feminists, and more likely to feel group identification (in the case of women) or group sympathy (in the case of men) with women than are nonvoters, Williams voters, or the national sample as a whole.

Over 80% of Richards voters consider themselves femi-

Claytie and the Lady

TABLE 5.5. Gender Consciousness in Texas and the Nation, 1991

	Texas Sample					National Sample
	Williams voters	Non- voters	Richards voters	Women	Men	All
	$N = 7$ %	$N = 17$ %	$N = 7$ %	$N = 17$ %	$N = 15$ %	$N = 465$ %
V2701: Attention to women in the news						
A lot	28.6	11.8	57.1	29.4	20.0	20.6
Some	42.9	35.3	28.6	29.4	46.7	42.8
A little	28.6	41.2	—	29.4	26.7	27.5
Not at all	—	11.8	14.3	11.8	6.7	9.0
V2714: Anger at women's treatment						
Most of the time	—	29.4	14.3	31.3	6.7	11.9
Some of the time	16.7	29.4	71.4	37.5	40.0	37.4
Occasionally	83.3	29.4	14.3	25.0	46.7	34.8
Almost never	—	11.8	—	6.3	6.7	16.0
V2706: Think of self as feminist?						
Yes	—	33.3	83.3	42.9	30.8	20.1
Don't use term	—	13.3	—	—	—	2.0
No	100.0	53.3	16.7	57.1	69.2	77.9
V2708: How women improve position						
Individual effort	50.0	47.1	—	43.8	28.6	42.7
Work together	50.0	52.9	100.0	56.3	71.4	57.3
V2713 (women only): Sense of pride in other women?						
Most of the time	66.7	36.4	100.0			36.4
Some of the time	33.3	36.4	—			33.5
Occasionally	—	27.3	—			20.9
Almost never	—	—	—			9.2

Source: American National Election Panel Study/pilot study, 1991.

nists, in comparison with a third of nonvoters, only a fifth of the national sample, and *none* of the Williams voters. *All* Richards voters stress the necessity of group action to better women's position, while roughly only half of the other groups take a group orientation. Richards voters pay the most attention to women in the news, and are angriest at women's treatment in society. Among female respondents, *all* Richards voters say they "take pride in the accomplishments of other women" at least most of the time. Although it is possible that the smallness of the Texas sample could produce such findings coincidentally, their consistency makes that unlikely, as do our theoretical and substantive expectations. In earlier chapters, we presented other evidence that Richards' candidacy had a stirring effect on women—sometimes stirring them to extreme dislike and discomfort, in the case of women who eventually voted for Williams. These findings seem to add to the evidence that for other women, particularly those women who voted for Richards, their own beliefs about women's rights to full roles in all of society, including the highest reaches of politics, found legitimation in Richards' candidacy.

And this was the case despite the fact that Richards' own feminism, while always known or assumed among the voting public, was not given a high profile in the campaign. As we have seen, the campaign organization sought and counted on women's support but without being overtly feminist or out of the "mainstream," and while at the same time assiduously wooing other groups. The practical, tactical qualities Ann Richards has always believed essential to effective politics would have prevented her from running as an idealistic feminist, even if she had been one. As Jane Hickie said, even after questions of women and feminism took on personal meaning for her, in the last of the "epiphanies" Hickie described, Richards was still as practical about coalition building as ever. Hickie put it this way: "Those principles, she was never uneasy again about the world of women's politics, or taking a position—there was never a question in the Governor's race [for example] on whether Ann Richards would be correct on [a pro-]choice [position]. I mean, that would have been nutty [to doubt her pro-choice stand]. [But] what we debated a lot was how to work with that in a political fashion" (interview, 21 November 1991). Or, as the Governor and Hickie both emphasized, neither sees much merit in running a hopeless race for the sake of "having your issues heard." Both think that the point is to win for the sake of being able to bring those issues to the table. The findings in Table 5.5 suggest most strongly that many women accepted Richards as one of their own, and did not appear to object that she was not running *only* as a woman. (See Appendix B for additional statistical evidence.)

In order to attempt further analysis, we combined the four questions asked of all respondents (excluding the women-only "pride in accomplishments" item) into a simple additive scale of "feminism." Each item was recoded, with non- or anti-feminist positions given negative numbers, neutral responses assigned to 0, and feminist or pro-woman responses given positive numbers. The resulting feminism scale has a potential range, then, of -6 to 6, with the least feminist respondents scoring lowest (or having the highest negative number score) and the most feminist respondents scoring highest. Its frequency distribution and coefficients of scalability are presented in Table B.2, where it is shown to be a sound and reliable measure. The relationship of the feminism scale to other affective and cognitive components is also presented. These components, all from the 1990 portion of the panel study, include affect toward the candidates (the Richards and Williams feeling thermometers), as well as cognitive considerations, represented by respondents' education in years and scores on the additive knowledge scale based on recognition of national and world political figures and knowledge of the partisan composition of the U.S. House of Representatives and Senate (see Appendix B).

We see in Table B.2 that, of the feminism items, attentiveness to women in the news is the most poorly connected to the scale as a whole (paralleling Americans' general inattentiveness to politics), but substantive considerations overrode purely statistical ones in our decision to retain it. We also see that the scale itself is positively associated with affect toward Richards and negatively associated with affect

TABLE 5.6. Regression of Vote Choice on Affective and Cognitive Measures in the Texas Sample, 1991

	Standardized regression coefficient
Education	-.037
Williams thermometer	-.009
Knowledge	.101
Richards thermometer	.402
Feminism scale	.278
R^2	.318

Source: American National Election Panel Study and 1991 pilot study. Note that individual regression coefficients, and the equation as a whole, are not statistically significant estimators of population parameters. Coefficients should be taken as suggestive only of relationships within the subsample upon which the analysis was done.

toward Williams, as we would expect to be the case. More surprisingly, the scale is negatively associated with knowledge. But recall that the level of knowledge in the sample as a whole is quite low, given its reliance on questions about international leaders, and questions of individual salience and relevance no doubt arise here. That is to say, in Texas at least, being a feminist certainly doesn't guarantee that one is very familiar with the international political scene. And many Texans would no doubt wonder why they *should* be familiar with it, if it has no obvious bearing on their day-to-day lives. The feminism scale is also inversely related to education in this tiny sample, no doubt reflecting the generally lower levels of education among Texas Democrats than among Republican Texans. Since we have seen that there is neither a moderate nor a "liberal" wing in the Texas Republican party, the relationship between feminism and education may also reflect an inverse relationship between feminism and Republican identification in Texas. In Texas, Republican women, like Republican men, are more likely to be comparatively affluent and well-educated, but less likely to be feminist, than are Democrats, as is very much more true among Republican men (none of whom, in the authors' personal experience, have ever claimed feminism as a top priority; recall, too, that an unprecedentedly large number of Republican women deserted their party in order to vote for Ann Richards, and they may well have taken most of Texas' Republican feminism with them). If we could risk looking at these relationships separately for each sex, that is what we would see; but statistical principles forbid us from doing so.

Table 5.6 presents the results of a regression of the vote in 1990 (ranging from -1 for a vote for Clayton Williams, to 0 for nonvoters, to 1 for a vote for Ann Richards). Readers are once again warned that the equation cannot be said to represent population parameters. In this case, the "population" in question consists of no more than our respondents themselves. For these respondents, the analysis tells us that, all other things being equal (and the regression accomplishes this by holding "other things" mathematically constant as it evaluates each separate item in the equation), their feelings about Ann Richards and their feminism (or anti-feminism) told us more about their voting behavior than did their educational levels, their abstract political knowledge, or even their reactions to Clayton Williams. Feminism, identification with women, and identification with Ann Richards probably do not constitute the whole of the voting decision for many people. But it is also true that, for women and for liberal men, in different and similar ways, Ann Richards' candidacy bore considerable weight. The fact that not only was she *running*, but she actually appeared capable of *winning*, must for many have resulted in the elating combination of practical purpose and affirmative ideals that characterizes the Governor's own approach to political life.

TELLING TEXANS APART

Can we tell the "engaged and angry," "the remote ones," and the "modest hopefuls" apart in meaningful ways? We assume, of course, that attentiveness to and participation in politics should readily separate the voters from the nonvoters, but how can Williams and Richards voters be distinguished from each other? And might this discrimination among groups work differently for women than it does for men? Our previous inquiries have led us to hypothesize that, beyond philosophical differences over policy or evaluations of the system, gender-role beliefs played a key role in the 1990 Texas gubernatorial election. Thus, we conducted three discriminant analyses[5] of the American National Election Study data—one for all respondents and one each for men and women—using our measures of political engagement and knowledge, federal spending preferences, ideological self-placement, feeling thermometers for the women's movement, Williams, and Richards, and the query about how much sex discrimination women face. We conducted an additional discriminant analysis of the exit-poll data as another check on the validity of what we have found. Since the election studies and the exit-poll questionnaires do not ask the same questions, we were forced to use different measures. But the two analyses complement each other well. Finally, in order to produce the most parsimonious and efficient results for our small numbers of cases, we ran a discriminant analysis on the exit-poll data again, but allowing only the most powerfully discriminating variables to remain in the analysis.

In each case, the two discriminant functions resulting from each analysis do a good job of assigning respondents to their correct groups; our calculations of Goodman and Kruskal's Tau for the classification tables show that the models produce substantial proportional reductions of error. That is, knowing only respondents' answers to the various questions, could we correctly assign them to their voting group? The models allowed us to do so a good deal more accurately than if we had assigned people to groups by, say, the toss of a coin. As we see in Table 5.7, the first function (or equation) of the analysis most obviously separates voters from nonvoters, while the second function separates Williams voters from Richards voters. Overall, federal spending preferences, judgments on the political system, internal political efficacy, and, to a lesser extent, reactions to Richards and to the women's movement contribute to the distinction among groups. There

Claytie and the Lady

TABLE 5.7. Discriminant Analyses of Williams Voters, Nonvoters, and Richards Voters, by Sex

Unstandardized function coefficients:	Function 1	Function 2
Discriminating variables		
A. Whole sample:		
Participation	.661	.492
Federal spending	-.051	.153
Attentiveness	.669	.441
System evaluation	.120	.293
Internal efficacy	.111	.216
Richards thermometer	-.034	.001
Women's movement thermometer	.007	.028
% Correct classification:		
Williams voters	73.3	
Nonvoters	78.8	
Richards voters	73.3	
Goodman & Kruskal's Tau	.521	
B. Men:		
Participation	.812	.225
Attentiveness	.679	.181
Richards thermometer	-.044	.008
Women's movement thermometer	.023	.043
% Correct classification:		
Williams voters	55.6	
Nonvoters	84.8	
Richards voters	69.2	
Goodman & Kruskal's Tau	.500	
C. Women:		
Participation	-.345	.581
Federal spending	.257	.150
Attentiveness	-.376	.785
Internal efficacy	.086	.756
Richards thermometer	.025	.013
% Correct classification:		
Williams voters	100.0	
Nonvoters	81.8	
Richards voters	70.0	
Goodman & Kruskal's Tau	.550	

Source: 1990 American National Election Study. Stepwise discriminant analysis (method = Wilks). Goodman & Kruskal's Tau calculations are by the authors.

are, however, meaningful differences in the ways the analysis performs for men and women. For men, Richards herself and reactions to the women's movement are most important. Differences in ideological preferences—views about federal spending, acknowledgment of sex discrimination, or ideological self-placement—seem unimportant. Nor does system evaluation or internal efficacy matter.

For women, in contrast, federal spending preferences and internal efficacy matter a good deal. The analysis of women alone is also rather more difficult to interpret. Attentiveness and participation seem to separate not only voters from nonvoters, but Williams voters from Richards voters, with the latter somewhat more politically engaged. A dislike of increased federal spending *and* a dislike of Ann Richards characterizes Williams voters. With Richards' "modest hopefuls," on the other hand, a preference for increased federal spending is joined to greater internal political efficacy to set them apart as a group.

The complexity of the analysis for women mirrors the complexity of women's emerging political lives. For men, as gender politics scholars have long argued and as this analysis appears to confirm, issues of gender and feminism can often be abstract, just another part of their general political outlook. In the 1990 gubernatorial election, men were in part turning thumbs up or down on Ann Richards as a representative of the "new woman." For women, though, she doubtless caused considerable speculation about their own lives. Williams voters, the angry ones, don't like the way things are going in society and, as Molly Ivins discovered as she followed the campaign, many women saw Richards as an invalidation of their own more traditional lives (interview, 14 May 1991). For Richards supporters, the campaign represented valorization, instead of threat: their own growing internal efficacy was reflected in her candidacy. We can also see that sensitivity to the complexity associated with gender politics today is the best route to understanding it. Despite the greater intricacy of the model for women, it was by far the most successful at classification.

The discriminant analyses of exit-poll data shown in

TABLE 5.8. Discriminant Analyses of Male and Female Williams and

Unstandardized Function Coefficients:	Function 1	Function 2
Discriminating variables		
A. Socioeconomic status and basic political orientations:		
Presidential vote, 1988	1.161	.447
Partisanship	.706	.413
Ideology	.318	-.079
Education	.006	.268
Country on right track	.316	-.403
Strong feminist	.317	-2.253
Abortion attitudes	.281	.010
Age group	-.038	.218
Family income	-.021	.125
Deciding issue: education	.156	-.521
Deciding issue: ethics	.251	-.049
Deciding issue: gun control	-.267	1.748
Deciding issue: abortion	-.020	-.730
Deciding issue: crime/drugs	-.521	.110
Deciding issue: state taxes	-.264	.829
Deciding issue: state economy	-.171	.710
% Correct classification:		
Women Williams voters	53.7	
Men Williams voters	55.0	
Men Richards voters	51.4	
Women Richards voters	40.2	
Goodman & Kruskal's Tau	.521	

Source: Voter Research and Surveys 1990 General Election Exit Poll: Texas file. Stepwise discriminant analysis (method = Wilks). Goodman & Kruskal's Tau calculations are by the authors.

Table 5.8 produced similar results. The functions that the analysis produced separated voters first by partisanship (because women were so much more likely to be Democratic and men so much more likely to be Republican), ideology, and sociotropic evaluations of the nation's well-being. Also contributing to the distinction were concerns about crime, drugs, abortion, and ethics, as well as about family income. The analysis strongly separates *male* Williams voters from *female* Richards voters—these two groups are much more

Richards Voters

Unstandardized Function Coefficients:	Function 1	Function 2

B. Traits of campaign and candidates:		
Whose campaign most negative?	1.390	
Candidate's experience	1.057	
Candidate's toughness	-.757	
Candidate as manager	-.086	
Opponent out of touch	.521	
Opponent too extreme	-.087	
% Correct classification:		
Women Williams voters	47.8	
Men Williams voters	50.2	
Men Richards voters	31.9	
Women Richards voters	51.2	
Goodman & Kruskal's Tau	.258	
C. Most parsimonious combined model:		
Presidential vote, 1988	.950	
Partisanship	.798	
Ideological self-placement	.255	
Candidate experience	.677	
Country on right track	.165	
Candidate toughness	-.688	
% Correct classification:		
Women Williams voters	49.0	
Men Williams voters	58.5	
Men Richards voters	31.7	
Women Richards voters	57.2	
Goodman & Kruskal's Tau	.320	

different from one another in their attitudes and opinions than are *female* Williams and *male* Richards voters—and the second function contributes to the distinction by separating men and women on the question of feminism. In general, we would have to say that the various approaches we have used to understand the gender politics of the 1990 Texas gubernatorial election, whether historical and cultural or involving assessment of elite judgments or analysis of survey data, have converged to tell a single, but highly intricate, story.

Claytie and the Lady

VOTER PORTRAITS

Clayton Williams' most likely voter is a young, conservative, fairly well-educated white man who is opposed to abortion. He says that he voted for George Bush in 1988, but he doesn't trust government. He is hostile to it, in fact, believing that it wastes money and opposing government spending on most issues—although he, like Claytie, would like to teach drug pushers the "joys of bustin' rocks." He seems fairly angry at the way the world is, perhaps for this reason valuing Claytie's "toughness" more than any other characteristic, although even he didn't like Claytie by election day as much as he had at the beginning. Even so, he likes Claytie more than he likes feminists or the women's movement, and he likes Ann Richards least of all.

Ann Richards' most likely voter is a pro-choice woman in early middle age, perhaps white, but also quite possibly African- or Mexican-American. She is not quite as well educated as is the average man. But she is interested in politics. She calls herself a Democrat, and she believes government should be taking an active role in solving social problems. She is modest, though, about the political roles she can play. She supports the women's movement, believes that women must work together, and may even call herself a feminist. She is proud of the accomplishments of other women, and very proud of Ann Richards. She was appalled by Claytie.

These are stereotypes, of course, drawn from statistical analyses. White, Black, and brown men voted for Richards, as did a surprising number of affluent, well-educated, white Republican women—but white women also voted for Williams. But if there is such a thing as a modal voter for each candidate, the portraits above represent those modal voters. The portraits make it clear that this race was a classic struggle over visions of government and society, over "New" versus "Old" Texas. What gives one pause is the degree to which "New" Texas came to be symbolized by a woman, while "Old" Texas was represented by a man. Never in the history of America's largest states, and certainly not in national politics, had such a crystallization occurred in an actual election—never had sex and gender been freighted with such political significance. Ann Richards was, no doubt, the same as *any* statewide elected official—any Treasurer, any Attorney General or any Lieutenant Governor—in that if she had not set her sights on the Governor's Mansion some years before she actually ran for Governor, her staff and supporters would have tried to set those sights for her. She, too, could look in the mirror each morning and see there, perhaps, the face of a Governor of Texas. The extraordinary aspect of the story is that so many others could look at her face and also see a Governor, a woman Governor. The most important part of the story, and the whole purpose of all the campaign strategies, all the individual voting decisions, is the choice of someone to govern. And it is with some reflections on Ann Richards' governing that we will end our telling of the tale.

You know, the ten-second sound bite is the manipulator . . . they want to use words that sound good but don't particularly communicate. They want to take the cautious approach, because I think the thing men fear the most is being laughed at. And the press is pretty brutal. Well, they can laugh at me all they want to. Just as long as they get it on the front page [she chuckles slyly] . . . I think . . . the day I was elected, my opposition or negative numbers were like fifty-one percent. The best part about it was that Clayton Williams' were higher. So my job obviously was to come in here and convey to the public that it's okay, I'm here now, you can trust me, I'll do a good job. And now those negatives are, I don't know where they are now, very low, they're down in the twenties. And does that bother me? Not particularly, no, it doesn't. They didn't elect me to be loved, they elected me to get a job done. And you don't get into jobs like this for your emotional gratification. You've got to have that somewhere else.

—GOVERNOR ANN RICHARDS, interview with the authors, 16 October 1991

Gender and Governing

Ann Richards is the first woman to be elected Governor of Texas entirely in her own right. She is the first "authentic liberal," in Chandler Davidson's terms, to have been elected Governor in Texas, all the more remarkable to have occurred at a time when "liberal" was more of a pejorative in Texas politics than it had been for twenty years. She is a woman of her times, in that her feminism and gender consciousness developed only after "epiphanies" of realization and intro-spection, of questioning and changing both her public and private roles. She is also a woman ahead of her times, in that her public roles, and her successes, may well stimulate epipha-nies in other Texas women.

More prosaically, her own electoral success certainly en-hances the credibility of other women candidates. We believe that Kay Bailey Hutchison, the Republican State Treasurer elected to fill the unexpired portion of Lloyd Bentsen's term in the U.S. Senate, and the first woman ever to represent Texas there, was such a beneficiary. She has been referred to often since 1990 as "the Republican Ann Richards"—many thought that she would be Richards' opponent in the 1994 gubernato-rial election—although, in fact, the two women bear almost no resemblance to one another in style, and even less in po-litical beliefs. But Hutchison was certainly able to take ad-vantage of Texas' apparent new receptivity to women candi-dates for the highest public offices. Her victory over Richards' appointee Bob Krueger, whose campaign was criticized as ineffectual, was a political embarrassment to the Governor, who could not retain the seat for the Democrats (although

Claytie and the Lady

she appointed a Democratic woman, Mayor Martha Whitehead of Longview, Texas, to succeed Hutchison as Treasurer). But, ironically, without the Governor's own historic victories in statewide offices, Hutchison would not have been seen as the viable candidate that she was. Hutchison must run again to retain her seat in the 1994 general election, and was, at the time of writing, facing a grand jury investigation into allegations that she misused staff time and resources at the State Treasury and then destroyed the evidence of having done so (White 1993). These charges were greeted with disinterest when the hapless Krueger raised them in the special election campaign, and were later reviled by Republicans as a Democratic conspiracy. If the charges had brought a conviction, the "Republican Ann Richards" would have had a brief career. They did not, and her reelection campaign is certain not to feature the kind of stark debates over sex and gender that so dominated the 1990 gubernatorial race: Hutchison's sex, or indeed any talk of a "woman's perspective," was virtually invisible in the special election, where she ran on a simple "no new taxes" platform. For that, for a freedom from having to establish one's competence, even one's *right* to run, that few women in the past have enjoyed, Hutchison can thank Richards, no matter with what wry irony each woman might regard such an expression of gratitude (Berke 1993; Verhovek 1993b, 1993c, 1993d; Ward 1993a, 1993b).

But this special election was not the only reason that the spring and early summer of 1993 were difficult for Governor Richards; in May she had suffered another defeat in the failure at referendum of her plan for refinancing Texas public elementary and secondary education. Few turned out in the election, called on 5 June, and of the 20% of eligible voters who did go to the poll, Hutchison captured a commanding 67.3% of their votes. Republicans immediately claimed that her victory was a referendum on both President Clinton and Governor Richards, while the truth is more likely to be that Democrat Krueger simply ran a poor campaign and was, in any case, not a charismatic figure. Even after the June special election, which followed the previous defeat for the Governor in May, Richards' approval ratings remained high.

School-finance reform had been a constant source of frustration for the Governor, with Texas, under court order, unable to find a solution that redressed the yawning imbalance of resources between the richest and poorest districts, even after twenty-five years of struggling over the issue. The Governor's proposal, called the "Robin Hood Plan" by its opponents, would have permitted poorer districts to levy charges against wealthier ones, and its defeat in the May referendum election was a stinging blow. Only twenty-four hours before a court deadline that would actually have shut down the Texas public schools on 31 May, the relieved Governor signed a bill emerging from an exhausted legislature that would, essentially, do what the "Robin Hood Plan" would have done (Verhovek 1993a; Graves 1993), significantly reducing the disparity between poor and rich districts' spending on education.

Equity in school systems' expenditures for their pupils may, to the uninitiated, seem to be a straightforward question. But for the Governor it was a grinding preoccupation for much of the second half of her term. The last-moment legislation, averting the closing of schoolhouse doors, was not the result of the brilliant vision of a leader, to which all gratefully responded; it was, instead, the result of conflict, selfishness, genuine philosophical difference, and recalcitrance . . . against which the Governor could pit little more than her own political instincts and willingness to compromise. The solution restored a good deal of her beleaguered political prestige, but at considerable cost. She has been able to achieve other modest improvements and changes, as with her appointment of "Skip" Meno as Education Commissioner. Meno shares the Governor's views about local control of public schools, greater accountability in public elementary and secondary education, and more state advocacy for teachers. Meno's vigorous agenda for public education has received widespread legislative and popular support (Brooks 1993), and the Governor's appointment of him signifies her desire to make good on her campaign promise to improve Texas schools. But the continuing problems associated with financing those schools are so massive that they overshadow other educational reforms.

We have seen how women and many men have responded to Ann Richards, not so much perhaps as a person—although her personal qualities do strike people—but more as a symbol of change: change in gendered political roles, and change, perhaps, in political leadership and in the empowerment of people. The two examples above make clear how well-nigh impossible it is for one person to revolutionize a political system or make everything happen as she would wish. Nonetheless, Richards and her constituents have had high expectations for her leadership from the beginning (Copelin 1991a). She had earlier said that the joy of having power was in giving it away, empowering others. She has used her appointment powers to do that, by, for example, bringing unprecedented numbers of women of all races and minority men into state government (Garcia 1992a), and by using her influence to bring clean water to the colonias of South Texas. Both of these things are important, and both are easier to accomplish than school-finance reform. But nothing is easy. Even bringing a clean water supply to the South Texas colonias has been slow and tedious, with less obvious and immediate progress than the frustrated Governor and the underserved citizens would have wished. Similarly, while the inclusion of drug-treatment programs in plans to build new prisons honors a campaign promise about which the Governor has felt strongly, political wisdom, however, indicates that Texans prefer to hear about the numbers of new prisons being built, not the drug treatments those new prisons will provide. She must attempt to lead in a far-from-unconstrained environment. What else can we say of the nature of that leadership?

Richards' orientation to leadership seems markedly different from the personally aggrandizing nature of power so very much a feature of Texas politics in the twentieth century. While so many of Texas' most notable political figures appear to have been motivated primarily by their own ambition for continuing power, from "Farmer Jim" Ferguson to Lyndon Johnson to William Clements, Richards seems unusually unstirred by thoughts of personal glory, although she obviously has the ego and ambition necessary to make and win high-stakes races. But from her days as an energetic, activist housewife to the present, she seems most moved by wanting to get things done. When we asked her what she thought the most essential qualities of leadership were, this is what she said:

> *I've always thought that it was very complicated. That it meant that whatever it is that you want to do has to be tied up with a very neat ribbon around a package, that you've got to know exactly what your goals are, who are the people who can do it, and you call up everybody and you all sit at the table, and you pass out assignments, and it's kind of like all the homework is assigned, and then you go back and check to make sure that everybody did what they were supposed to do, 'til you get there. That's what I thought leadership was. And it turns out it's not nearly that complicated . . . Leadership is knowing what you want, and then communicating it to the right people. And it's really not much more difficult than that. When you achieve a position of responsibility, people are very anxious to try to carry out what you want to do. They endow you with power whether you have it or not. So I suppose I think that my own qualities are that I do know what I want. On any given subject. And I usually have a pretty good instinctive knowledge about how to get it.*

"Knowing what she wants," for Ann Richards, is neither principally a matter of personal power for herself (she does, however, care about her reelection), nor, certainly, is it a dreamy idealism about reinventing the world. The commitment to justice that she absorbed in her youth and her later feminism both represent ideals, but ideals that she pursues in an utterly unromantic, pragmatic way:

> *A lot of us think that we have to have all the answers. We don't have to have them, but we have to want them. And we have to be willing to admit that we don't know if we've done everything right or*

> not. We've just done the best we can. And then,
> when you've done that, well, you pray to God it will
> be enough. There are just a lot of things I know
> about politics, and some I've known from instinct
> and some I've known from practice. But the rule of
> thumb to me is, if you can't win a race, why make
> it! Don't give me a bunch of garbage about how you
> think issues ought to be discussed, because if you
> and your issues get defeated, you haven't done
> anything but spend somebody's money, and take up
> everybody's time. I think another rule of thumb is
> that unless you have something to say that is going
> to catch the emotion of the people, not just the
> imagination, but the emotion, their gut feeling, well
> then you're not communicating. And we see a lot of
> that in politics now. My feeling is that a lot of these
> young men run and emulate the dull guys they've
> seen before so, you know, you've got a lot of old
> guys serving, with these new dull guys coming after
> them. And the American public's just bored to tears.
> (Interview, 16 October 1991)

Whatever the Texas public has been, it has not been not bored by Ann Richards. All of what we have found points to the same conclusion and is supplemented by continued evidence, such as a poll in 1991 finding that Democrats of both sexes and Republican women think women are underrepresented in the state legislature (Texas Poll 1991: 8), or polls in September of 1992 and July of 1993 showing Richards' approval rating ranging from 73% to a still hefty 58%, with broad support from almost all groups (Slater 1992, 1993). Increasingly, feminist and gender-conscious Texans want more women in office not only as a matter of justice but for the changes they believe women will make in politics, and even those who are neither feminist nor gender-conscious have high expectations for women in office—and especially for Ann Richards. Many are counting on Governor Richards to demonstrate the changes that women will supposedly bring to politics, to the nation, and to the world.

As we write, the Governor has completed three-quarters

of her first term in office, and has withstood both of the legislative sessions falling within that first term, as the state legislature will not convene again until after the 1994 elections. Many observers, even among Republicans, believe that she will have a second term. She is likely to face only token opposition, if that, in the Democratic primary. In a refreshing change from the constant money worries she faced in the 1990 campaign, her 1994 campaign organization begins with a war chest of some three million dollars even before the reelection campaign is seriously under way. Her likely Republican opponents are only now exploring the viability of their candidacies, and know that they will face a popular incumbent (Attlesey 1993; Diehl 1993).

The Republican race was brought into sharp focus by the entry into it of George W. Bush, the managing partner of the Texas Rangers baseball team and eldest son of the former President. Bush, known fondly by Republicans as "George the Younger" or "Little George," and not so fondly by Democrats as "Boy George" or "Shrub," formally announced his candidacy on 8 November 1993, after having speculated about making a run for sufficiently long to dampen the enthusiasm of other GOP contenders. At this writing, the odds favor Bush to win the Republican nomination. While the younger Bush refuses to discuss comparisons with his father, a Richards-Bush race surely creates vintage Texas electoral theater, in which the son attempts to vindicate his father against the woman who, in 1988, said that that father had been born "with a silver foot in his mouth."

Results from an October 1993 Texas Poll, before Bush had declared his candidacy, found Richards ahead "if the election were held today" by a margin of 47% to 39%, with 14% undecided. The same poll revealed the Governor's "favorable" rating to stand at 61%, while Bush began his candidacy in an unusually strong position for a challenger, provided that not too many poll respondents had confused him with his father, who won Texas in the 1992 presidential election (Attlesey 1993a).

But "George the Younger" has never held public office, and his sole previous foray into electoral politics on his own behalf was a failed bid for a Texas seat in the U.S. House of Representatives in 1978. His initial public appearances in aid of his candidacy included general criticisms of Governor Richards' record on crime, education, and the state budget—all perennial Texas favorites about which he offered few specific proposals; against the criticisms, the Governor's campaign speedily mounted a vigorous defense. But Bush claimed that the Governor's record did not merit her reelection, and indeed her record will form part of voters' judgments about her (Attlesey 1993b; 1993c; Elliot 1993).

How will her incumbency be judged? What have her successes and failures been, and how have people seen them through the prisms of gender? We cannot, nor do we want to, accomplish a systematic review of all her actions as Governor in this space. School-finance reform and the election of Kay Bailey Hutchison are two events that have stood out, however, along with a number of other significant issues. They all must be understood in the context of Texas politics, and with regard for Ann Richards' personality and fundamental approach to politics.

First, the Texas political culture is (with apologies to Chandler Davidson, upon whose work we have often relied in these pages) quite conservative or, at the very least, it is adamantly resistant to sweeping changes in social and economic policy making. Texans may complain about their bottom-basement rankings in provision of health services, or welfare, or education, but they will not tax themselves to remedy those conditions, as their resounding rejection of the "Robin Hood Plan" showed. Texans do not like "big government," and scorn the idea that activist government can do good. The Texas legislature, despite the many powerful and entrenched legislators there, is not considered to be "professional"; indeed, the high jinks in the legislature (often more its business than policy making, it seems) have brought disbelieving laughter more than admiring approval.

Ann Richards, the "authentic liberal," faces all these obstacles to any significant change she wishes to make. She is further hampered by the fact that the Texas Governor's powers are among the weaker of the powers of American Governors. She has significant appointment powers, and has used them very shrewdly to effect changes in the "face" of state government, as well as in its policies. She had promised in the campaign that her appointments would reflect the demographic composition of Texas, and within her first year she achieved that goal. Of her first 650 appointments, 48% were female, 25% were Hispanic, and 12% were Black. The Governor said that "the difference that [these appointments] make is that the dialogue changes when everyone is seated at the table," and that " . . . it is the right thing to do . . . it is the smart thing to do" (Attlesey 1991). This use of her appointment power was clearly a smart thing for the Governor to do, allowing her to accomplish three purposes simultaneously. First, she was able to act on principles of equality and justice to which she has hewed during her entire political career. Second, she was able to honor a campaign promise. Finally, her appointments would help to provide continuing political mobilization of two groups that had supported her election in 1990, namely, women (of all races) and minority men.

But since her formal powers are relatively weak, Richards, like any Texas Governor, must hope that she can exert considerable informal influence. This she has done, getting high marks for a "hands-on, win-win" approach to her dealings with the legislature (Slater 1991). Her creative use of appointment powers, both to reform state agencies and to bring women and minority men "to the table," as well as her intensely personal, accessible style with state legislators, have enabled her to keep a number of the campaign promises she made. She faces enormous constraints, however. She is, for example, on the record as a strong environmentalist, as demonstrated by her legislative agenda and her appointments. She has also promised to spur Texas' economic growth by creating a hospitable climate for business, and to improve the wages and working conditions of poorer Texans. Those goals can all too easily clash (Garcia 1992b), and the formal powers of her office are not in themselves strong enough to help her avoid such dilemmas. Nor even is her "control" of the Democratic party and its likely core of voters extensive, as the special Senate election made all too clear.

Would Ann Richards nonetheless be a "transformational" leader? In James MacGregor Burns' (1978) classic formulation, mere "transactional" leadership occurs "when one person takes the initiative in making contact with others for the purpose of an exchange of valued things . . . But beyond this the relationship does not go." Transformational leadership, in contrast, "occurs when one or more persons *engage* with others in such a way that leaders and followers raise one another to higher levels of motivation and morality . . .]T]ransforming leadership ultimately becomes *moral* in that it raises the level of human conduct and ethical aspiration of both leader and led, and thus it has a transforming effect on both" (pp. 19–20; emphasis in original). Transformational leadership is a large and profound thing, but this is what many have hoped Ann Richards would provide.

Of course, in many ways her leadership is transformational because she is there, because a woman is governing, with no "Pa" issuing the real decisions from the boudoir. She herself sees some differences in women's leadership from that of men:

> *Well, I can't know, but my guess is that there will always be a difference. You know, just like men, we're not all alike. I can name some really rotten women office holders. They're not dishonest, but they're not very good. So I think, just because we're different, does not necessarily mean that we are better. So presently I think we work harder because it's been harder for us to get there, but that may be temporary . . . [On the other hand], we're more conditioned to consensus-building, I think, than men are. We have less experience at team play than men do, but I think that by nature we are more conciliatory and less abrasive. We don't particularly enjoy the fight, and I think some men do. I think our natural instincts are to find a solution. (Interview, 16 October 1991)*

A number of her opponents would disagree that she is more conciliatory or less abrasive, and stories of the Governor's temper make it clear that indeed she *has* the temper we would expect of anyone as strong and impatiently goal-directed as she is. "She doesn't put up with incompetencies, no matter what kind of gender it comes in," as one of the Governor's associates told us.

And she *is* impatiently goal-directed. She is no ideologue or dreamer. Jane Hickie says:

> *She recognizes the fact that she, first, is the Governor of Texas, and Texas has an agenda of needs and wants. And those are not the same, sometimes, as what the priorities would be for a women's organization. Or—that's not right . . . I mean, here's an example . . . Ann Richards' position on the space station or supercollider is "I've got to have it for Texas. And I'm going to evaluate my help to you politically based on whether you help me on my stuff over here." She's comfortable being at the table; she's not an advocate anymore. She is the Governor. (Interview, 21 November 1991)*

Richards is the object of Progressives', reformers', and even some feminist groups' bitter disappointment—bitter because, after all, an "authentic liberal" had been elected at last, but the revolution did not come, and disappointed because she *does* compromise and "deal," and because she is highly skilled at using her power within the existing rules of the game. (For examples of such disappointment, see Cullen 1992; *Texas Observer* 1992; Burka 1993; for an even-handed analysis of such reactions, see McNeely 1993.)

Perhaps nowhere was the disappointment more evident than in the case of reform of state and political ethics rules, where she was deemed to have done far less than she should have, to which she replied that the only Ethics Commission that would please her critics was "one that descended from the heavens with angels singing" (Copelin, 1991b). Here we see the *old* gender role stereotypes operating upon *new* political roles for women: Does not everyone expect that women will hold the unimpeachably highest moral and ethical standards? The difficulty here, as it was for Victorian suffragettes, is that such a simplistic, and gendered, view does not comport comfortably with a belief that women, too, can do "real-world" politics. And "real-world" politics, for a Governor with comparatively weak formal powers, means that almost always, less will be accomplished than might have been.

The Governor as well as some of her disappointed supporters also suffered when her protégée, Lena Guerrero, whom Richards had appointed to the powerful Texas Railroad Commission (regulating oil and gas), was confronted with evidence that she had lied about graduating from college. Guerrero, who was running for reelection to the seat to which Richards had appointed her, apologized but initially seemed unrepentant. Sources close to the Governor told us privately that Richards was greatly angered by Guerrero's deceit and that Guerrero was strongly "advised" to consider resignation. Barbara Jordan, the Governor's ethics advisor and one of the most esteemed figures in Texas politics, publicly chastised Guerrero in the sternest terms at a press conference, suggesting that such deceit made one unsuitable to serve the public trust.

While Richards did not formally withdraw her endorsement of Guerrero in her reelection bid, she made herself more and more distant. The Governor's distress and displeasure were evident (Hight 1992; Hoppe 1992). Guerrero's behavior was *surely* not a "new" or "woman's" way of leading; to most Texans, it seemed like "politics as usual." Certainly male political elites had suffered similarly shattering scandals. However disappointed Richards may have been with Guerrero, she is too pragmatic to think such cases cannot arise among women as well. Her appointment of former Employment Commissioner Mary Scott Nabers to another vacancy on the Texas Railroad Commission (created by Bob Krueger's appointment to the U.S. Senate) and her appointment of former Longview Mayor Martha Whitehead as Treasurer (following Kay Bailey Hutchinson's election to the Senate) can be seen as strong symbolic reaffirmation of her "everyone at the table" approach to Texas state government, Guerrero's lapse notwithstanding.

In Chapter 2, and implicitly throughout the entire book, we have seen a woman who would rather leave the table with *something* than with nothing except her ideals. This is simply the way the Governor sees politics:

*And what matters most to me is that I be able to
determine what I feel are the priorities of this state*

that demand my personal attention, and lay out a
strategic plan to achieve them. That's not that much
different from the way you run a [campaign], and
the planning process, and the laying out of a strat-
egy, the activities to accomplish . . . [but] my role
now as Governor is to follow through on commit-
ments I made as a candidate, to embrace those
people who were not necessarily my friends in the
campaign, not for political purposes but for purposes
of advancing my programs, and bringing those
disparate groups together that can bring about
change. (Interview, 16 October 1991)

Yet Richards is forthright about her visions. Insurance
reform, for example, hardly seems revolutionary, but it has
economic, health, and legal consequences for thousands of
Texans, and she has been uncompromising in her demands
for closer scrutiny and regulation of the insurance industry
(Slater and Moreno 1993). Taking on the insurance industry
was an oft-repeated campaign promise, and she intended to
keep that promise. Her approach to insurance coverage and
rates has been vigorously consumer oriented. In fact, her efforts in this area have been among her boldest and most
conflictual, as she confronted an enormously wealthy and
politically entrenched (if admittedly unpopular) interest.
While her own Insurance Board appointees recommended that
they be replaced with a single Insurance Commissioner, many
observers saw the industry-backed structural and policy legislation of the 1993 session as a setback for the Governor.
But with her appointment of J. Robert Hunter, known as the
"founder" of the national insurance consumer movement,
as Insurance Commissioner (Eskenazi 1993), she appeared to
have trumped her adversaries. It is difficult to make insurance reform exciting (or understandable) to the average voter,
and the Governor has made few friends in the insurance industry. For Ann Richards, though, it is just the kind of battle
that she promised to undertake to make government function for its citizens. Even the crusty and very progressive *Texas*
Observer, for whom little is ever liberal enough, credits the
Governor with keeping "progressives involved in negotiations

as much as possible" and notes that she used her powers of influence, and the veto, adroitly to protect consumer, environmental, health, and public service issues (Dubose and Cullen 1993).

And there is a delight in fighting the good fight. Mary Beth Rogers, Richards' old friend and first Chief of Staff, told us unself-consciously of the *joy* of governing:

> *So the joy that you get, you know, you've been in campaigns where you win, or you lose, and it's a joy, or an instant sadness, but then you go on, you forget that. But these [dearly cherished policies such as water for the South Texas colonias or new beds for drug treatment] are things that somehow have the ability to last, and to outlast you. And so there's a different sense of contentment in that. And then there's always the next problem around the corner . . . (Interview, 15 October 1991)*

Governor Richards has also addressed "women's issues" and has acted on her identification with women. She is proud of the "anti-stalking" bill that she shepherded through the legislature and signed into law (Garcia 1993). She has remained uncompromising in her pro-choice stand on abortion; her promise to veto any restrictive bill has preempted serious pro-life legislative activity (Hoppe and Kilday 1992). And, after eighteen years as a counselor at Girls' State, the program that had been so important to the young Ann Willis, Governor Ann Richards escorted the Girls' State Governor to the younger Governor's swearing-in ceremony. "It was incredible to be sworn into office with Texas' woman Governor looking on," Girls' State Governor Maryana Iskander said (Graves 1992).

And it does seem incredible. Ann Richards rose to the Governor's Mansion against what seemed like impossible odds. She is an extraordinarily vivid "symbolic woman." She is the repository of hopes and of disappointments. She is tough, and pragmatic, and she loves the give and take of real politics. She is transformational, and she is transactional. And there is always the next problem around the corner.

List of Interviews

Adams, Kirk. Richards' deputy campaign manager and son-in-law. Interviewed in person by Jeanie R. Stanley, 14 August 1991, Austin, Texas.

Hickie, Jane. Director, Texas Office of Federal Relations. Interviewed in person by Sue Tolleson-Rinehart, 21 November 1991, Washington, D.C.

Ivins, Molly. Journalist. Interviewed in person by Sue Tolleson-Rinehart and Jeanie R. Stanley, 14 May 1991, Austin, Texas.

Masset, Royal. Director of Research, Texas Republican party. Interviewed in person by Sue Tolleson-Rinehart and Jeanie R. Stanley, 13 May 1991, Austin, Texas.

Masset, Royal. Second interview, on telephone, by Jeanie R. Stanley, 22 December 1992, Austin, Texas.

McKinnon, Mark. President, McKinnon Media (Democratic media and campaign consultants). Interviewed in person by Sue Tolleson-Rinehart and Jeanie R. Stanley, 14 May 1991, Austin, Texas.

Richards, Ann. Governor of Texas. Interviewed in person by Sue Tolleson-Rinehart and Jeanie R. Stanley, 16 October 1991, Austin, Texas.

Rister, Milton. Political Consultant, Texas Republican party. Interviewed on telephone by Sue Tolleson-Rinehart, 3 August 1993, Chapel Hill, North Carolina.

Rogers, Mary Beth. Chief of Staff, Governor's Office, January 1991–August 1992. Interviewed in person by Sue Tolleson-Rinehart and Jeanie R. Stanley, 15 October 1991, Austin, Texas.

Rove, Karl. President, Rove and Company (Republican campaign consultants). Interviewed in person by Sue Tolleson-Rinehart, 14 October 1991, Austin, Texas.

Shipley, George. Shipley and Associates (Democratic campaign consultants). Interviewed in person by Sue Tolleson-Rinehart and Jeanie R. Stanley, 14 May 1991, Austin, Texas.

Smiley, Martha. Attorney and Richards fundraiser. Interviewed in person by Sue Tolleson-Rinehart and Jeanie R. Stanley, 13 May 1991, Austin, Texas.

Treat, Jennifer. Finance Director, Richards campaign. Interviewed in person by Sue Tolleson-Rinehart, 15 October 1991, Austin, Texas.

Weeks, David. President, Media Southwest (Republican campaign consultants). Interviewed in person by Sue Tolleson-Rinehart, 14 October 1991, Austin, Texas.

Coding of Variables for Scale Creation in the 1990 American National Election Study

A. *Knowledge:* V395–V401 are whether R knows the job/position of Dan Quayle, George Mitchell, Mikhail Gorbachev, Margaret Thatcher, Nelson Mandela, Tom Foley, respectively. V402–V403 are whether R knows who held the most seats in the Senate and House before the 1990 election. Variables were recoded as 1 = R correctly recognizes and 0 = R incorrectly recognizes or won't guess, and were summed. True range = 0 to 9.

B. *Attentiveness:* V62, interest in the campaign, recoded as 1 = very or somewhat interested, 0 = not interested. V63, V65, V68 are dichotomous—following campaign in newspapers, watching campaign programs on TV, and discussing politics with family/friends, recoded as 1 = did, 0 = did not. Variables were summed. True range = 0 to 4.

C. *Participation:* V166, V366–V369, V371 are dichotomous variables measuring whether R (respondent) voted in 1988, tried to influence others, used a button/bumper sticker, attended a political meeting, worked for a party/candidate, or gave money to a candidate, respectively. Variables were recoded as 1 = did, 0 = did not, and were summed. True range = 0 to 6.

D. *System evaluation:* V504–V507 are: "can trust the government in Washington," recoded as 1 = most or all of the time, 0 = a lot; "people in government waste money," recoded as 1 = not much or some, 0 = a lot; who government benefits, recoded as 1 = benefit of all, 0 = benefit of a few big interests; and "people in government crooked," recoded as 1 = hardly any or not many, 0 = quite a few. Recoded variables were summed. True range = 0 to 4.

E. *Internal efficacy:* V508–V510 are Likert scale, measuring "public officials don't care what people like me think," "people like me have no say in what government does," and "sometimes politics is too complicated." Variables were recoded as -1 = strongly agree or agree, 0 = neither agree nor disagree, 1 = strongly disagree or disagree. True range = -3 to 3.

F.   *Federal spending:* V377–V387 are the preferences for federal spending in the order in which they appear in Table 5.3. They were recoded as -1 = decrease federal spending, 0 = same, 1 = increase federal spending. True range = -11 to 11.

G: *Other variables:* V406, liberal/conservative self-placement, was recoded as -1 = conservative, 0 = moderate, 1 = liberal. V461, how much sex discrimination women face on the job, was reverse-coded as 1 = none, 3 = some, 5 = a lot. Feeling thermometers were used in their original form.

TABLE B.1. Frequencies and Scalability of Scales

	Knowledge %	Attentive %	Participation %	System %	Efficacy %	Spending %
-6						1.6
-5						.8
-4						1.6
-3					28.5	.8
-2					11.7	4.9
-1					25.5	4.1
0	19.4	6.3	34.5	28.2	9.5	6.6
1	14.6	13.3	41.0	25.8	17.5	8.2
2	18.8	16.8	12.9	17.7	3.6	10.7
3	15.3	30.8	7.9	19.4	3.6	9.0
4		13.2	32.9	1.4	8.9	10.7
5		9.7		2.2		9.8
6		5.6				9.0
7		1.4				12.3
8		.7				6.6
9		1.4				2.5
10						.8
Mean	2.6	2.7	1.1	1.6	-.99	3.3
N	144	143	139	124	137	122
Alpha	.754	.565	.614	.600	.494	.710

Source: 1990 American National Election Study. "Alpha" is Cronbach's Alpha coefficient of scalability.

TABLE B.2. The Feminism Scale in the Texas Sample, 1991

Valid Percentage

A. Scale distribution

-4	8.3
-3	8.3
-2	16.7
-1	8.3
0	12.5
1	4.2
2	8.3
3	16.7
4	4.2
5	8.3
6	4.2
N of cases	24
Chronbach's alpha	.487

B. Item-to-total correlation

Attention to women in news	.029
Angry at women's treatment	.597
Think of self as feminist	.125
How women improve position	.547

C. Correlation of feminism scale to other cognitive and affective measures

	Richards thermometer	Williams thermometer	Knowledge	Education
Feminism scale	.391	-.341	-.290	-.220
Richards thermometer		-.039	-.167	-.106
Williams thermometer			-.240	-.136
Knowledge				.539

Notes

PROLOGUE: THE MEANING OF THE 1990 GUBERNATORIAL RACE

1. It is very fashionable of late to replace all uses of the term "sex" with "gender." Historically, such a replacement occurred in order to avoid the embarrassment of stimulating thoughts of the sex act as well as of biological sex. Today, such replacements are a misguided attempt to acknowledge that, indeed, gender differences are probably more significant to us as we struggle to figure out men's and women's places in the world than is the difference of mere biological sex. But the attempt remains misguided for a number of reasons. First, in politics, we need to ask questions about both virtual *and* substantive representation. We are interested in *how many* women hold elective office, for example, because such a question of virtual representation has its own weighty ramifications for justice and democratic theory. When we ask those "how many" questions, though, we are asking questions about sex, not gender. But because gender roles are constructed from, and upon, biological sex, questions of substantive representation come into play: Are we not also concerned about "how many" women there are because we expect women to make some sort of difference, to lead differently, to bring different policy questions to the public agenda, or to offer alternative solutions to the policy questions already on the agenda? Implicitly, somehow, most of us have this expectation. Nonetheless, the difference between sex/virtual representation and gender/substantive representation should not be obscured. Not the least of our considerations in recognizing the difference is that when the differences *are* obscured, that is tantamount to saying that all public women are "everywoman," that differences *among* women have very much less meaning than do differences *between* women and men. The conflation of sex and gender is evident in the problematic

reification of "difference" (not "differences") characterizing so much of contemporary feminist theory (for a thorough critique, see Hawkesworth 1990). At a more practical level, Ann Richards, for example, can and does stand as a virtual representative of women, and she may well offer a different kind of substantive representative, too. But she is not "everywoman," and many women would disagree that she represents them at all. What we are arguing for here is a continued embrace, hard as that is, of the thorny intricacies that both sex and gender create in politics.

1. GENDER AND TEXAS POLITICAL CULTURE IN THE TWENTIETH CENTURY

1. Ann Richards, in contrast, has kept Texas and the nation laughing through the use of her own sharp wit, and not as the butt of the wit of others. Surely this, too, in its way, is emblematic of some genuine change in society's orientations toward, and acceptance of, public women.

2. THE EDUCATION OF A PUBLIC WOMAN

1. As readers will see in the subsequent discussion, we are heavily indebted to Chandler Davidson's (1990) trenchant work of political sociology and political history, *Race and Class in Texas Politics*. Davidson tries to argue that Texans are, in fact, a good deal more likely to be liberal than is commonly realized, and he correctly takes Fehrenbach and others to task for creating what are virtual caricatures of Texas politics, allowing little scope for any appreciation of the genuine diversity of Texans. But while we applaud Davidson's outstanding achievement, we are also political scientists with long experience in the conundrums of mass survey research on political orientation and ideologies. Davidson's argument that Texans are not overwhelmingly conservative rests to a considerable extent on analysis of 1968 data from the Comparative State Elections project. His analysis of respondents' ideological self-placement (their description of themselves as "liberal," "middle-of-the-road," or "conservative") prompts him to conclude that Texans are about as moderate as the nation as a whole, and no more conservative than, for example, Minnesotans (see pp. 38–39). But, as political scientists have known and worried about for years, we have miserably little evidence that "average" people attach much

meaning, beyond some vague symbolic representations, to phrases such as "liberal" and "conservative" (see, as just three among countless studies, Smith 1989; Conover and Feldman 1981; Conover and Feldman 1984). Being aware of what we don't know—we don't know what respondents "know" when we ask them to use these terms—we certainly cannot make the leap to assuming that we know Texans and Minnesotans are using the terms to mean the same thing, if indeed they attach much meaning to them at all. We think that outcomes of recent elections and referenda, and Davidson's own gloomy conclusions about Texas' abysmal social welfare policy making (see pp. 270–271), lead instead to the conclusion that most Texans remain resistant to change in the social and economic policy status quo. This resistance has significant implications for the impact Ann Richards' governing can have on the state, as we discuss further in the epilogue.

2. Davidson notes that it was not until 1982 that "four liberals" won second-tier statewide offices (p. 179). One of those four liberals was Ann Richards, in her first race for the State Treasurer's office.

3. The exhilarated relief that greeted Richards' election was partly compounded of the expectation that she would be both strong and activist on the one hand, and *colorful* (but not too embarrassingly colorful, as Williams would have been) on the other. Texans had come to miss gubernatorial theater, something they had not seen much of since John Connally's time. This relish can be seen in the *Texas Monthly* article "Ann of a Hundred Days," published after her first three months in office. It crows that "[f]or the first time in goodness-knows-when, Texas has a real governor. In case you've forgotten after all those years of [Richards' predecessors] Preston [Smith] and Dolph [Briscoe] and Mark [White] and Bill [Clements], a governor is supposed to have a vision for the state, a program to carry it out, and the political skills and personal popularity to see it through. For the time being, at least, Richards has them all" (Burka 1991: 128).

4. The electoral system mentioned refers to a system of single-member districts where the winner takes all; for this reason scholars find that women are often more successful in multimember or party list proportional representation systems–where they may also be able to avoid "negative campaigning." Incumbency advantage harms women, of course, because most incumbents are male, but it should be noted that, once they can become incumbents, women enjoy all the same advantages. The "value" of the office has traditionally harmed women candidates because they face more obstacles

to receiving or winning party nomination to highly competitive, well-compensated, and/or prestigious office, and because, should they get the nomination, they are then quite likely to face male incumbents. This helps explain why women are more likely to be found in offices of lower value all the way up the political ladder: women are more likely to be mayors of smaller rather than larger cities, and women are more likely to be in lower rather than upper legislative chambers, especially in the U.S. Congress (see, for example, Darcy, Welch, and Clark 1987; Welch and Studlar 1990; and consider that in 1992, the "Year of the Woman," the vast majority of women who were successful in U.S. House and, particularly, Senate races were running for "open" seats, where no incumbent was running).

3. CAMPAIGN STRATEGIES

1. This is a charge frequently laid against women's campaigns. The evidence suggests that women's campaigns are no less professionally run or strategically competent than are men's (Carroll 1985; Darcy, Welch, and Clark 1987), but because women have often been disadvantaged by running against incumbents, and have had fundraising difficulties in the past, they have done things that are not, perhaps, immediately recognized as successful by those who cleave to the political orthodoxy.

2. Many observers greet this explanation with cynical disdain, but in our experience, this is a sincere and common reaction of recovering alcoholics to such disclosure questions, especially for those who have used the Alcoholics Anonymous program, as had Ann Richards.

4. THE UNFOLDING OF A GUBERNATORIAL CAMPAIGN

1. In this, we think the Texas gubernatorial race offers a much better model for understanding what credible female presidential candidates will face than do the models drawn from legislative races, or from races for lower office generally. The higher the stakes of the office, the less easy it will be to talk benignly of women's cooperative, collegial, "nurturant" leadership styles. Women may have all these traits—we know many women elites who demonstrate them daily—but the most valuable and prestigious political offices have

been bitterly fought over, and we do not believe that women candidates will be spared any of the bitterness.

5. GENDER ROLES AND GENDER POLITICS

1. The data in this chapter are drawn from the Texas file of Voter Research and Surveys 1990 Exit Poll (VRS is the consortium of the ABS, CBS, NBC, and CNN television networks that pooled resources to conduct a single exit poll on 6 November), the 1990 American National Election Study, Texas Sample, and the American National Election Study 1990–1991 panel study of the political consequences of war/pilot study. The number (N) of cases for the Texas file in the exit-poll data is 2,648. Ns of cases for the two American National Election Study data sets are discussed in the text.

2. "Feeling thermometers" are devices long employed by the American National Election Study investigators to measure the degree of emotional warmth or coolness toward a variety of political groups and persons, such as the President, feminists, or "poor people." Respondents are shown a list of groups, and are also shown a picture of a thermometer. They are asked to estimate how "warm" or "cool" they feel about each person or group on the list by giving a thermometer reading. From 0 to 49 degrees falls within the range of coolness; 50 degrees indicates complete emotional neutrality; and from 51 to 100 degrees indicates progressively warmer feelings. As can be seen in Table 5.4, and as one would expect, both Ann Richards and Clayton Williams stimulated more intense reactions from voters than did most other groups—Clayton Williams, in fact, was viewed with more "coolness" than was any other group on the list except "pro-abortion groups."

3. A "panel study" in survey research refers to a study in which the *same* people are interviewed repeatedly, but at least twice, at different points in time. Such studies are valuable because they allow us genuinely to examine possible changes in attitudes and opinions within the same person—in this case, the attitudes of people before and after the Persian Gulf War—rather than across different samples of people, in which case individual-level change can only be inferred. But for our purposes, the panel study is especially valuable because it gives us a chance to examine people's feminism a year after the Texas gubernatorial race.

4. The new gender measures can be found as V2701–V2733 of Pilot Form Two in the 1991 study.

5. Discriminant analysis is a statistical technique that assembles various combinations of independent variables (knowledge, feeling-thermometer scores, and the like) until it finds the best "cut point" below which one group falls, and above which falls another. In this way, it can find the best way to separate groups mathematically, and can then assign as many members as possible to their correct groups. In botany, discriminant analysis might be used to determine how different two kinds of trees are by examining such characteristics as the veining pattern and shape of leaves, the color of bark, and the like (the "independent variables"). In our case, the "trees" are people, and the "leaf shapes and bark colors" are attitudes. If people who vote for one candidate have attitudes that are sufficiently different from those who vote for another candidate or who don't vote, then knowing those attitudes alone ought to let us use discriminant analysis to "predict" which voting or nonvoting group people belong to. In this way, we are not actually predicting people's membership in one of the groups as much as we are trying to figure out which of the attitudes matter most in telling the groups apart. We get the final "most parsimonious model" by using a stepwise method minimizing Wilks' lambda, allowing only those independent variables that can make a truly significant separation between groups to enter the equation.

Selected References

Alexander, Deborah, and Kristi Andersen. 1991. "Gender Role Beliefs as Frameworks for Candidate Evaluation." Paper presented to the Annual Meeting of the Midwest Political Science Association. Chicago.

Andersen, Kristi. 1990. "Women and Citizenship in the 1920s." In Louise A. Tilly and Patricia Gurin, eds., *Women, Politics, and Change*. New York: Russell Sage Foundation.

Anderson, James E., Richard W. Murray, and Edward L. Farley. 1989. *Texas Politics*. 5th ed. New York: Harper & Row.

Attlesey, Sam. 1990. "Engendering Uneasiness." *Dallas Morning News*, 21 March, pp. 1A, 14A.

Attlesey, Sam. 1990a. "Williams Denounces Gift to Richards." *Dallas Morning News*, 20 July, p. 21A.

———. 1990b. "Richards Must Close Gap Fast, Experts Say." *Dallas Morning News*, 23 September, p. 1A.

———. 1990c. "Williams Defends '86 IRS Filing." *Dallas Morning News*, 4 November, p. 1A.

Attlesey, Sam. 1991. "Richards' Appointment Successes Worry Republicans." *Dallas Morning News*, 6 October, p. 44A.

———. 1993. "Mossbacher to Test Waters with Reform Book." *Dallas Morning News*, 8 August, p. 48A.

Attlesey, Sam. 1993a. "Poll Finds Bush is '94 Contender." *Dallas Morning News*, 24 October, pp. 1A, 9A.

———. 1993b. "Republican Hopeful Hints at How to Unseat Richards." *Dallas Morning News*, 7 November, pp. 43A, 51A.

———. 1993c. "George W. Bush Makes Gubernatorial Bid Official." *Dallas Morning News*, 9 November, pp. 1A, 9A.

Attlesey, Sam, and Wayne Slater. 1990. "Williams Didn't Pay Income Taxes in '86." *Dallas Morning News*, 3 November, p. 1A.

Beck, Paul Allen, and M. Kent Jennings. 1982. "Pathways to Participation." *American Political Science Review* 76(March): 94–108.

Beck, Paul Allen, and M. Kent Jennings. 1988. "Childhood Social-
    ization Environments and Adult Political Involvement." Paper
    presented to the Annual Meeting of the American Political Sci-
    ence Association. Washington, D.C.
Berke, Richard L. 1993. "Clinton Coattails Debated After Senate
    Loss in Texas." *New York Times*, 7 June, pp. A1, A10.
Bowman, Ann O'M. 1984. "Physical Attractiveness and Electability:
    Looks and Votes." *Women & Politics* 4(Winter): 55–65.
Brooks, A. Phillips. 1993. "School Chief Meno Tackles Status Quo."
    Austin American-Statesman. 7 November, pp. B1, B5.
Brown, Norman D. 1984. *Hood, Bonnet, and Little Brown Jug: Texas
    Politics, 1921–1928.* College Station: Texas A&M University
    Press.
Buechler, Steven M. 1990. *Women's Movements in the United
    States: Woman Suffrage, Equal Rights, and Beyond.* New
    Brunswick, N.J.: Rutgers University Press.
Burka, Paul. 1991. "Ann of a Hundred Days." *Texas Monthly.* May:
    126–134.
Burka, Paul. 1993. "Sunrise, Sunset." *Texas Monthly.* May: 7–10.
Burns, James MacGregor. 1978. *Leadership.* New York: Harper
    Torchbooks.
Carli, Linda L. 1990. "Gender, Language, and Influence." *Journal of
    Personality and Social Psychology* 59(5): 941–951.
Carroll, Susan J. 1985. *Women as Candidates in American Politics.*
    Bloomington: Indiana University Press.
Carroll, Susan J. 1989. "Gender Politics and the Socializing Impact
    of the Women's Movement." In Roberta Sigel, ed., *Political
    Learning in Adulthood: A Sourcebook of Theory and Research.*
    Chicago: University of Chicago Press.
Cartwright, Gary. 1991. "Who Says One Man Can't Change the
    World?" *Texas Monthly.* September: 103–104, 160–167.
Center for the American Woman and Politics. 1991. "Women in
    Elective Office 1991" fact sheet. New Brunswick, N.J.: Rutgers
    University.
Conover, Pamela Johnston. 1988a. "'So Who Cares?' Sympathy and
    Politics." Paper presented to the Annual Meeting of the Mid-
    west Political Science Association. Chicago.
Conover, Pamela Johnston. 1988b. "Feminists and the Gender Gap."
    Journal of Politics 50(November): 985–1010.
Conover, Pamela Johnston, and Stanley Feldman. 1981. "The Ori-
    gins and Meaning of Liberal/Conservative Self-Identifications."
    American Journal of Political Science 25(November): 617–645.
Conover, Pamela Johnston, and Stanley Feldman. 1984. "How People

Organize the Political World: A Schematic Model."*American Journal of Political Science* 28(February): 95–126.

Conover, Pamela Johnston, and Virginia Sapiro. 1992. "Gender, Feminist Consciousness, and War." Paper presented to the Annual Meeting of the Midwest Political Science Association. Chicago.

Cook, Alison. 1993. "Lone Star." *The New York Times Magazine*, 7 February: 22–38.

Copelin, Laylan. 1990. "Abortion Battle Looming Over State Republican Convention." *Austin American-Statesman*, 22 June, p. A1.

Copelin, Laylan. 1990a. "Williams Speaks and Jaws Drop." *Austin American-Statesman*, 12 July, p. B6.

Copelin, Laylan. 1990b. "Richards Camp Vows to Unmask Williams." *Austin American-Statesman*, 3 August, p. B2.

Copelin, Laylan. 1990c. "Lost: Yellow Dog, Votes Democrat." *Austin American-Statesman*, 17 September, p. A1.

Copelin, Laylan. 1990d. "With Gaffe, Williams Denies Cut in Poll Lead." *Austin American-Statesman*, 29 September, p. B1.

Copelin, Laylan. 1990e. "Drug-use Issue Rises Again in Governor's Race." *Austin American-Statesman*, 20 October, p. A1.

Copelin, Laylan. 1991a. "A New Texas Nears its 100th Day."*Austin American-Statesman*, 21 April, p. A1.

Copelin, Laylan. 1991b. "Ethics Gap: Texas, Florida Responded in Different Ways." *Austin American-Statesman*, 27 October, pp. A1, A22.

Costantini, Edmond, and Kenneth H. Craik. 1977. "Women as Politicians: The Social Background, Personality, and Political Careers of Female Party Leaders." In Marrianne Githens and Jewel Prestage, eds., *A Portrait of Marginality*. New York: David McKay.

Cott, Nancy F. 1987. *The Grounding of Modern Feminism*. New Haven, Conn.: Yale University Press.

Cott, Nancy F. 1990. "Across the Great Divide: Women in Politics Before and After 1920." In Louise A. Tilly and Patricia Gurin, eds., *Women, Politics, and Change*. New York: Russell Sage Foundation.

Crawford, Ann Sears, and Crystal Sasse Ragsdale. 1982. *Women in Texas: Their Lives, Their Experiences, Their Accomplishments*. Austin, Tex.: Eakin Press.

Cullen, James. 1992. "Taking Stock of the Vote." *Texas Observer*, 27 November, p. 8.

Darcy, R., Susan Welch, and Janet Clark. 1987. *Women, Elections and Representation*. New York: Longman.

Davidson, Chandler. 1990. *Race and Class in Texas Politics.* Princeton, N.J.: Princeton University Press.

Deaux, Kay, and Brenda Major. 1987. "Putting Gender Into Context: An Interactive Model of Gender-Related Behavior." *Psychological Review* 94(July): 369–389.

Deaux, Kay, and Brenda Major. 1990. "A Social Psychological Model of Gender." In Deborah L. Rhode, ed., *Theoretical Perspectives on Sexual Differences.* New Haven, Conn.: Yale University Press.

Diehl, Kemper. 1993. "GOP Upbeat, but Governor Ready." (Opinion/Editorial.) *San Antonio Express-News.* 25 July, p. 2–M.

Dubose, Louis, and James Cullen. 1993. "73rd Legislature Observed." *Texas Observer,* 16 July, pp. 10–13.

Duverger, Maurice. 1955. *The Political Role of Women.* New York: UNESCO.

Elliot, David. 1993. "George W. Bush Makes Pitch in Bid to Strike Out Richards." *Austin American-Statesman,* 7 November, pp. A1, A12.

Elshtain, Jean Bethke. 1987. *Women and War.* New York: Basic Books.

Eskenazi, Stuart. 1993. "Longtime Adversary of Insurers Takes Office as State's Top Regulator." *Austin American-Statesman,* 4 November, pp. A1, A14.

Fehrenbach, T. R. 1968. *Lone Star: A History of Texas and the Texans.* New York: Macmillan.

Flexner, Eleanor. 1973. *Century of Struggle: The Women's Rights Movement in the United States.* New York: Atheneum.

Flick, David. 1990. "Absentee Tally Tipped County Democrats to Richards Win." *Dallas Morning News,* 24 November, p. 34A.

Fowlkes, Diane L., Jerry Perkins, and Sue Tolleson Rinehart. 1979. "Gender Roles and Party Roles." *American Political Science Review* 73(September): 772–780.

Frankovic, Kathleen. 1982. "Sex and Politics—New Alignments, Old Issues." *PS* 15(Summer): 439–448.

Fraser, Antonia. 1990. *The Warrior Queens: The Legends and the Lives of Women Who Have Led Their Nations in War.* New York: Vintage Books.

Garcia, James E. 1992a. "Richards Record of Appointments is One of Diversity." *Austin American-Statesman,* 9 February, pp. A1, A17.

Garcia, James E. 1992b. "Environment, Economy Clash, Posing Conflict for Richards." *Austin American-Statesman,* 18 March, pp. B1, B4.

Garcia, Kimberly. 1993. "Austin Man First Jailed Under New Stalking Law." *Austin American-Statesman*, 30 March, pp. B1, B4.

Germond, Jack, and Jules Witcover. 1990. "Texas 'Runaway' Becomes a Horserace." *National Journal*, 27 October, p. 2618.

Gillman, Todd J. 1990. "Gender Gap Key in Governor's Race." *Dallas Morning News*, 4 November, p. 30A.

Graves, Debbie. 1991. "Despite Some Defeats, Session Pleases Richards." *Austin American-Statesman*, 29 May, p. A1.

Graves, Debbie. 1992. "Richards Encourages Girls' State Attendees." *Austin American-Statesman*, 23 June, p. B3.

Graves, Debbie. 1993. "Governor Signs School Bill, Sends It to Judge." *Austin American-Statesman*, 1 June, p. A7.

Gravois, John. 1990a. "Abortion Looms as Issue That Could Divide GOP." *Houston Post*, 23 January, pp. A1, A10.

Gravois, John. 1990b. "Williams Paid Prostitutes as Youth." *Houston Post*, 22 April, p. A1.

Griffith, Dotty. 1993. "EMILY'S List Sets a Record." *Dallas Morning News*, 27 January, pp. 5C, 16C.

Haavio-Mannila et al. 1985. *Unfinished Democracy: Women in Nordic Politics*. Trans. Christine Badcock. New York: Pergamon Press.

Hamilton, Arnold. 1980. "Texas Talks." *Dallas Morning News*, 28 October, p. 28A.

Hawkesworth, Mary E. 1990. *Beyond Oppression: Feminist Theory and Political Strategy*. New York: Continuum.

Hight, Bruce. 1992. "Jordan Says If Guerrero Wins She Should Quit." *Austin American-Statesman*, 22 October, pp. A1, A15.

Hoppe, Christy. 1992. "Guerrero Blasts Williams: Ex-candidate Said Her Race, Sex Got Her Job." *Dallas Morning News*, 20 October, pp. 19A, 26A.

Hoppe, Christy, and Ann Marie Kilday. 1992. "Stage Set for Battle in Legislature: Richards Vows Veto of New Restrictions." *Dallas Morning News*, 30 June, pp. 1A, 8A.

Huddy, Leonie, and Nayda Terkildsen. 1993. "Gender Stereotypes and the Perception of Male and Female Candidates." *American Journal of Political Science* 37(February): 119–147.

Huddy, Leonie, and Nayda Terkildsen. 1993a. "The Consequences of Gender Stereotypes for Women Candidates at Different Levels and Types of Office." *Political Research Quarterly*. 46(3): 503–525.

Ivins, Molly. 1990. "Cast Your Vote—But Not For the Wrong Don Yarborough." *Dallas Times Herald*, 6 November, p. A–11.

Ivins, Molly. 1991. *Molly Ivins Can't Say That, Can She?* New York: Random House.

Ivins, Molly. 1993. "Holy Debacle, What an Electoral Massacre." *Texas Observer,* 18 June, p. 2.

Jamieson, Kathleen Hall. 1992. *Dirty Politics: Deception, Distraction, and Democracy.* New York: Oxford University Press.

Jennings, M. Kent. 1979. "Another Look at the Life Cycle and Political Participation." *American Journal of Political Science* 23(November): 755–771.

Jennings, M. Kent, and Barbara G. Farah. 1981. "Social Roles and Political Resources: An Over-Time Study of Men and Women in Party Elites." *American Journal of Political Science* 25(August): 462–482.

Jennings, M. Kent, and Gregory B. Markus. 1984. "Partisan Orientations over the Long Haul: Results from the Three-Wave Political Socialization Panel Study." *American Political Science Review* 78(December): 1000–1018.

Jennings, M. Kent, and Richard G. Niemi. 1981. *Generations and Politics.* Princeton, N.J.: Princeton University Press.

Kay, Michele. 1990. "Corporate Texas Not Uneasy With New Governor." *Austin American-Statesman,* 8 November, p. B5.

Kelso, John. 1990a. "On Home Field, Richards Plays to No Advantage." *Austin American-Statesman,* 4 October, p. A1.

Kelso, John. 1990b. "Claytie Country: Fort Stockton Stands Behind Hometown Candidate." *Austin American-Statesman,* 16 October, p. A1.

Key, V. O., Jr., with Alexander Heard. 1949. *Southern Politics in State and Nation.* New York: Alfred A. Knopf.

Kidder, Louise H., Michelle A. Fagan, and Ellen S. Cohn. 1981. "Giving and Receiving: Social Justice in Close Relationships." In Melvin J. Lerner and Sally C. Lerner, eds., *The Justice Motive in Social Behavior.* New York: Plenum Press.

Kirkpatrick, Jeane J. 1974. *Political Woman.* New York: Basic Books.

Kuempel, George. 1990. "Williams Ad Seeks to Offset Verbal Gaffes." *Dallas Morning News,* 3 November, p. 33A.

Kuempel, George, and Wayne Slater. 1990. "Statement: Williams' Bank Acted Illegally." *Dallas Morning News,* 12 October, p. A11.

Lasher, Patricia, and Beverly Bentley. 1980. *Texas Women: Interviews and Images.* Austin, Tex.: Shoal Creek Publishers.

Lodge, Milton, Kathleen A. McGraw, and Patrick Stroh. 1989. "An Impression-Driven Model of Candidate Evaluation." *American Political Science Review* 83(June): 399–419.

Lucchesi, Carol Young, and Pamela J. Edwards. 1993. "Explanations of Social Cognition and Power Dynamics: Implications for Women in Organizations." Paper presented to the Annual Meeting of the Midwest Political Science Association. Chicago.

McNeely, Dave. 1990a. "Richards Gets the Upper Hand in Handshake Skirmish." *Austin American-Statesman,* 16 October, p. A9.

McNeely, Dave. 1990b. "Votes of Women, Minorities, Made Richards' Day." *Austin American-Statesman,* 8 November, p. A20.

McNeely, Dave. 1993. "Fans, Foes Debate Sunset Advisory Commission's Worth." *Austin American-Statesman,* 25 March, p. A19.

Mandel, Ruth B. 1981. *In the Running: The New Woman Candidate.* New York: Ticknor and Fields.

Matthews, Glenna. 1992. *The Rise of Public Woman: Woman's Power and Woman's Place in the United States, 1630–1970.* New York: Oxford University Press.

Means, Marianne. 1990. "Williams' Callousness Negates Texas' Positive Image." *San Antonio Light,* 30 April, editorial page.

Morris, Celia. 1992. *Storming the Statehouse: Running for Governor with Ann Richards and Dianne Feinstein.* New York: Charles Scribner's Sons.

Murphy, Dean E. 1992. "Texan Leads Feisty Fund-Raiser for Boxer, Feinstein." *Los Angeles Times,* 21 October, p. A3.

Pierce, Patrick A. 1989. "Gender Role and Political Culture: The Electoral Connection." *Women & Politics* 9(1): 21–46.

Richards, Ann. 1989. *Straight from the Heart: My Life in Politics and Other Places.* New York: Simon & Schuster.

Rogers, Mary Beth. 1990. *Cold Anger: A Story of Faith and Politics.* Denton, Tex.: University of North Texas Press.

Rothschild, Scott. 1990. "Rape Victim Decries Joke by Williams." *Dallas Morning News,* 30 October, p. 9A.

Sapiro, Virginia. 1982. "If U.S. Senator Baker Were a Woman: An Experimental Study of Candidate Images." *Political Psychology* 3(Spring/Summer): 61–83.

Sapiro, Virginia. 1983. *The Political Integration of Women.* Urbana: University of Illinois Press.

Sapiro, Virginia. 1986. "The Gender Bases of American Social Policy." *Political Science Quarterly* 101(2): 221–238.

Sapiro, Virginia. 1990. "The Women's Movement and the Creation of Gender Consciousness: Social Movements as Agents of Change." In Orit Ichilov, ed., *Political Socialization, Citizen*

Education, and Democracy. New York: Teacher's College Press.

Sapiro, Virginia. 1993. "The Political Uses of Symbolic Women: An Essay in Honor of Murray Edelman." *Political Communication* 10(April–June): 137–149.

Scott, Ann Firor. 1984. *Making the Invisible Woman Visible.* Urbana: University of Illinois Press.

Sigel, Roberta, and Marilyn B. Hoskin. 1981. *The Political Involvement of Adolescents.* New Brunswick, N.J.: Rutgers University Press.

Sigel, Roberta, and Nancy L. Welchel. 1986. "Minority Consciousness and Sense of Group Power Among Women." Paper presented to the Annual Meeting of the Midwest Political Science Association. Chicago.

Slater, Wayne. 1990a. "Race Brings Out Worst About Hopefuls." *Dallas Morning News,* 30 October, p. 17A.

Slater, Wayne. 1990b. "Candidates Spar on Final Weekend." *Dallas Morning News,* 4 November, p. 1A.

Slater, Wayne. 1991. "Richards Makes Mark on Office." *Dallas Morning News,* 21 April, p. 1A.

Slater, Wayne. 1992. "Most Texans Rate Richards Highly, Poll Shows." *Dallas Morning News,* 7 September, p. 16A.

Slater, Wayne. 1993. "Richards' Popularity Still High." *Dallas Morning News,* 24 July, p. 33A, 39A.

Slater, Wayne, and Sam Attlesey. 1990. "Williams Fends Off Attacks After Fumbled Questions." *Dallas Morning News,* 1 November, p. 1A.

Slater, Wayne, and Joseph Garcia. 1990. "Williams Remark Called Despicable." *Dallas Morning News,* 22 September, p. 33A.

Slater, Wayne, and Sylvia Moreno. 1993. "Governor Vents Ire At Insurers." *Dallas Morning News,* 9 May, pp. 39A, 41A.

Smith, Eric R. A. N. 1989. *The Unchanging American Voter.* Berkeley: University of California Press.

Solomon, Barbara. 1984. *In the Company of Educated Women.* New Haven, Conn.: Yale University Press.

Spruill, Julia Cherry. [1938] 1972. *Women's Life and Work in the Southern Colonies.* New York: W. W. Norton & Company.

Stanley, Jeanie R. 1985. "Life Space and Gender Politics in an East Texas Community." *Women & Politics* 5(4): 27–49.

Stanley, Jeanie R., and Diane D. Blair. 1989. "Gender Differences in Legislative Effectiveness." Paper presented to the Annual Meeting of the American Political Science Association. Atlanta.

Suro, Roberto. 1990. "Richards Promises a New Direction." *New York Times,* 8 November, p. B2.

Swartz, Mimi. 1990. "Meet the Governor: Ann Richards." *Texas Monthly*. October: 119–166 (interrupted).

Taylor, Elizabeth A. 1987. *Citizens at Last: The Woman Suffrage Movement in Texas*. With photographs and documents. Austin, Tex.: Ellen C. Temple.

Texas Observer. 1990. "On the Governor's Race." 28 September, pp. 7–9.

Texas Observer. 1992. "UT Inc." 24 April, pp. 3–4.

Texas Poll. 1991. *The Texas Poll Report*. Vol. 8, No. 4(November). Austin, Tex.: Harte-Hanks Communication.

Thomas, Sue. 1991. "The Impact of Women on State Legislative Policies." *Journal of Politics* 53(November): 958–976.

Tolchin, Susan, and Martin Tolchin. 1974. *Clout: Womanpower and Politics*. New York: Coward, McCann & Geohegan.

Tolleson Rinehart, Sue. 1985. "Toward Women's Political Resocialization: Patterns of Predisposition in the Learning of Feminist Attitudes." *Women & Politics* 5(4): 11–26.

Tolleson Rinehart, Sue. 1987. "Maternal Health Care Policy: Great Britain and the United States." *Comparative Politics* 19(1): 193–211.

Tolleson Rinehart, Sue. 1989. "The Life Course and Intergenerational Change: A Brief Note on the Transmission of Political Roles From Mothers to Daughters." Paper presented to the Annual Meeting of the American Political Science Association. Atlanta.

Tolleson Rinehart, Sue. 1992. *Gender Consciousness and Politics*. New York: Routledge.

Tolleson Rinehart, Sue. 1994. "The California Senate Races: A Case Study in the Gendered Paradoxes of Politics." In Elizabeth Adell Cook, Sue Thomas, and Clyde Wilcox, eds., *Year of the Woman: Myths and Realities*. Boulder, Colo.: Westview.

Tyler, Tom R. 1986. "The Psychology of Leadership Evaluation." In Hans Werner Bierhoff, Ronald L. Cohen, and Jerald Greenberg, eds., *Justice in Social Relations*. New York: Plenum Press.

Tyler, Tom R., Kenneth A. Rasinski, and Kathleen M. McGraw. 1985."The Influence of Perceived Injustice on the Endorsement of Political Leaders." *Journal of Applied Social Psychology* 15(8): 700–725.

Verhovek, Sam Howe. 1993a. "Poor Would Tax the Rich in Texas Plan for Schools." *New York Times*, 28 May, p. A7.

Verhovek, Sam Howe. 1993b. "Punching at Shadows in Texas Contest." *New York Times*, 3 June, p. A8.

Verhovek, Sam Howe. 1993c. "From Demure Survivor to Republican Star: Kathryn Ann Bailey Hutchison." *New York Times,* 7 June, p. A10.

Verhovek, Sam Howe. 1993d. "Old Accusations Surround New Texas Senator." *New York Times,* 12 June, p. 7.

Ward, Mike. 1990. "Political Barbs Draw Blood." *Austin American-Statesman,* 12 October.

Ward, Mike. 1993a. "Richards to Announce Treasurer Appointee." *Austin American-Statesman,* 18 June, p. B1.

Ward, Mike. 1993b. "GOP Says Democrats Conspired to Discredit Sen. Hutchinson." *Austin American-Statesman,* 18 June, pp. B1, B2.

Ware, Susan. 1990. "American Women in the 1950s: Nonpartisan Politics and Women's Politicization." In Louise A. Tilly and Patricia Gurin, eds., *Women, Politics, and Change.* NewYork: Russell Sage Foundation.

Weddington, Sarah, Jane Hickie, and Deanna Fitzgerald. 1977. *Texas Women in Politics.* Edited by Elizabeth W. Fernea and Marilyn P. Duncan. Austin, Tex.: Foundation for Women's Resources.

Welch, Susan, and Donley T. Studlar. 1990. "Multi-Member Districts and the Representation of Women: Evidence from Britain and the United States." *Journal of Politics* 52(May): 391–412.

White, Jerry. 1993. "Hutchison's Lawyers Say Her Side of Story Awaits." *Austin American-Statesman,* 7 November, pp. A1, A12.

Wiesen Cook, Blanche. 1992. *Eleanor Roosevelt: Volume One, 1884–1933.* New York: Viking.

Author Index

Subject Index